MEALS IN MINUTES

Better Homes and Gardens

BETTER HOMES AND GARDENS CREATIVE COOKING LIBRARY, FOURTH PRINTING

©MEREDITH PUBLISHING COMPANY, 1963. ALL RIGHTS RESERVED

PRINTED IN THE UNITED STATES OF AMERICA

Pink Parfait Pie—your blender makes it fast

Shrimp Almond Sauce—fabulous freezer fix-up

Mixed Grill, a

In Butterscotch

FROZEN
BROCCOLI

FROZEN
SHRIMP
SOUP

speedy broiler specialty

Torte Supreme—mixes!

CAKE MIX

FROSTING MIX

PUDDING MIX

Contents

This seal means recipe goodness

Every recipe in this book is *endorsed* by *Better Homes & Gardens* Test Kitchen. Each one is tested over and over till it rates excellent in practicality, family appeal, ease of preparation, and deliciousness!

Better Homes *and Gardens* TEST KITCHEN

Short-cut cooking

Dinner in 45 minutes? It's possible!
The family will think you're a
wonder—and you are, with the help
of skip-a-step mixes and canned
foods, preparation pared to bare
essentials, no-cook ingredients.
Still delicious? Of course! Try our
wonderful recipes; invent your own—

Jiffy meal stars Big-wheel Burger Skillet—

It's really "meat loaf" cooked the quick way, with a speedy
topper of spicy canned spaghetti sauce and kidney beans. Cut
wedges and serve on toasty French bread. Salad's fast, too:
Cottage Cheese Relish, olives, sliced fresh vegetables.

Main dishes like magic

Big-wheel Burger Skillet

See this speedy "meat loaf" on page 6—

1 tablespoon instant minced onion
½ cup milk
1½ pounds ground beef
1 slightly beaten egg
½ cup quick-cooking rolled oats
2 teaspoons salt
¼ teaspoon coarsely ground pepper
Kitchen bouquet
1 8-ounce can (1 cup) spaghetti
    sauce with mushrooms
1 8-ounce can (1 cup) kidney beans
Buttered, toasted French bread slices

Soak onion in milk 5 minutes; mix in ground beef, egg, rolled oats, salt, and pepper. Mound in 10-inch skillet. With wooden spoon handle, score in 5 or 6 wedges. Brush top lightly with kitchen bouquet.

Combine spaghetti sauce and kidney beans (with liquid). Pour over meat mixture. Simmer uncovered 20 to 25 minutes or till done. Serve wedges on French bread slices; spoon sauce over. Serves 5 or 6.

One-step Tamale Pie

1 pound ground beef
1 cup chopped onion
2 cloves garlic, minced

• • •

2 8-ounce cans seasoned tomato sauce
1 cup milk
2 slightly beaten eggs
1 12-ounce can whole kernel
    corn, drained
½ cup sliced pitted ripe olives
Few dashes bottled hot pepper sauce
¾ cup yellow corn meal
2 to 2½ teaspoons chili powder
2 teaspoons salt

In large skillet, cook ground beef, onion, and garlic till meat is browned and onion is tender. Stir in remaining ingredients. Turn into 12x7½x2-inch baking dish.

Bake in moderate oven (350°) 45 minutes or till knife inserted comes out clean. Cut in squares. Makes 8 servings.

15-minute Stroganoff

good

1 pound round steak, ¼ inch thick
1 3-ounce can (⅔ cup) broiled
    sliced mushrooms, with liquid
1 envelope or can *dry* onion-soup mix
1 cup dairy sour cream
2 tablespoons all-purpose flour

Trim fat from meat and reserve. Cut meat diagonally across grain in very thin strips. Heat fat in skillet till you have about 3 tablespoons melted fat (if necessary, add butter); remove trimmings. Brown meat.

Add ⅔ *cup water* and mushrooms. Stir in soup mix. Heat to boiling. Blend sour cream and flour. Add to hot mixture. Cook and stir till mixture thickens—sauce will be thin. Serve over noodles. Serves 5 or 6.

Speedy Italian Supper

4 slices bacon
⅓ cup *each* chopped celery and onion
1 3-ounce can (⅔ cup) broiled
    sliced mushrooms, drained
1 1-pound can spaghetti
    in tomato sauce

Cook bacon crisp; drain, crumble. In 1 tablespoon of drippings, cook celery and onion. Add mushrooms, spaghetti. Heat to bubbling. Sprinkle bacon over. Serves 3.

Tamale Skillet Meal

½ cup chopped onion
1 1-pound can beef tamales in sauce
1 1-pound can cream-style corn
1 8-ounce can seasoned tomato sauce
½ to 1 teaspoon chili powder
1 cup shredded sharp process cheese
¼ cup sliced pitted ripe olives

In skillet, cook onion in 1 tablespoon butter till tender. Add *sauce* from canned tamales. Stir in next 3 ingredients, and salt and pepper to taste. Simmer uncovered 5 minutes. Add ½ *cup* of the cheese.

Cut tamales in half lengthwise; arrange cut side up atop corn mixture. Heat. Trim with remaining cheese and olives. Serves 4.

Mexican Chiletti

Cook ¼ cup chopped onion in 1 tablespoon butter. Stir in one 1-pound can spaghetti with sauce and one 10½-ounce can chili without beans. Heat through.

Top with ½ cup shredded sharp cheese. Spoon over crisp corn chips. Serves 4.

Dixie Dandy Bake (*See cover*)

1 1-pound can applesauce
¼ teaspoon ginger
2 12-ounce cans luncheon meat
1 8-ounce can pineapple slices
1 1-pound 2-ounce can sweet potatoes

• • •

½ cup apricot jam
½ teaspoon dry mustard
¼ teaspoon salt
1 tablespoon water

Combine applesauce and ginger; spread in 10x6x1½-inch baking dish. Slice each loaf of luncheon meat 3 times on the diagonal, cutting *only ¾ of the way through*.

Halve pineapple slices; insert in cuts in meat. Place meat atop applesauce; arrange sweet potatoes around meat. Combine remaining ingredients. Spread over meat, pineapple, and potatoes. Bake at 400° for 35 to 40 minutes. Makes 6 servings.

Skillet "Pizza"

1½ tablespoons fat
3 medium potatoes, pared
  and thinly sliced
Salt and pepper
½ cup chopped onion
½ cup chopped green pepper
2 cups julienne strips ham or canned
  luncheon meat (1 12-ounce can)

• • •

3 eggs
½ cup shredded sharp process
  American cheese

Melt fat in 10-inch skillet. Spread *half* the potato slices over bottom; sprinkle with salt and freshly ground pepper. Top with a layer of *half* the onion and *half* the green pepper, seasoning with salt and pepper. Arrange *half* the meat atop.

Repeat layers of vegetables, *reserving* the remaining meat for garnish.

Cover; cook over low heat till potatoes are tender, about 20 minutes. Break eggs into bowl; pour over potatoes, breaking yolks and spreading eggs evenly with a fork. Add meat, spoke-fashion. Cover and cook till eggs are set, about 10 minutes. Top with cheese; cover till cheese starts to melt, about 2 minutes. Center with parsley. Cut in wedges. Serves 5 or 6.

Add these ideas to your bag of tricks, and supper's a snap!

Squaw Corn is practically a whole meal in a skillet! Cube one 12-ounce can luncheon meat; brown cubes in a little hot fat.

Combine 3 slightly beaten eggs, one 1-pound can golden cream-style corn, ¼ teaspoon salt, and dash pepper. Add to meat.

Cook over low heat, stirring occasionally, just till eggs are set. Makes 4 servings.

Texas Chili—couldn't be easier! Avocado tempers the chili "burn."

Heat one 10½-ounce can chili without beans to bubbling. Peel 1 avocado; reserve a few thin slices for garnish. Dice remainder into chili; heat briefly. Pour into serving bowls and top with the reserved avocado. Pass crisp corn chips. Makes 2 servings.

Saucy Spaghetti in a Flash

1 8-ounce package spaghetti dinner
¾ pound ground beef

. . .

1 8-ounce can seasoned tomato sauce
1 8-ounce can spaghetti sauce
  with meat
1 3-ounce can (⅔ cup) broiled sliced
  mushrooms, drained

Cook spaghetti in boiling *unsalted* water according to package directions; drain.

Meanwhile, brown meat; drain off excess fat. To skillet add the envelope of seasonings from spaghetti dinner, the tomato sauce, spaghetti sauce with meat, and mushrooms. Cover and simmer 5 minutes. Spoon sauce over hot spaghetti. Serves 4.

Lazy-day Lasagne

It's a mighty good stand-in for the start-from-scratch kind, ruffly noodles and all—

4 ounces lasagne or wide noodles
¼ teaspoon oregano
1 15½-ounce can spaghetti sauce
  with meat
1 cup cream-style cottage cheese
1 6-ounce package sliced
  Mozzarella cheese

Cook noodles in boiling salted water following package directions. Drain. Combine oregano with spaghetti sauce.

In greased 10x6x1½-inch baking dish, alternate layers of noodles, cottage cheese, spaghetti sauce, and Mozzarella cheese slices. Bake in moderate oven (375°) about 30 minutes. Makes 4 servings.

Cheese Franks

1 pound (8 to 10) frankfurters

. . .

1 6-ounce roll process cheese food—
  pepper, garlic, smoky, or bacon
  flavor
1 3-ounce package corn chips,
  coarsely crushed (about 1 cup)

Split frankfurters lengthwise, cutting only about ¾ the way through. Place in a shallow baking dish or jellyroll pan. Spread cut surfaces with cheese food; sprinkle cheese generously with crushed corn chips. Bake in moderate oven (350°) until heated through, about 15 minutes. Serves 4 or 5.

Frank-'n-Noodle Supper

Supper's in a skillet! Just plan rolls and salad— that's all you'll need—

1 No. 2½ can (3½ cups) tomatoes
½ cup water
1 envelope spaghetti-sauce mix
1 cup chopped celery
1 tablespoon instant minced onion
1½ teaspoons sugar
6 frankfurters
2 tablespoons butter or margarine
4 ounces (3½ cups) medium noodles
½ cup shredded sharp process
  American cheese

For sauce, combine first 6 ingredients. Cut franks in thirds diagonally; brown in butter. Add the noodles; pour sauce over, moistening all.

Cover; cook over low heat, stirring occasionally, 25 minutes or till done. Sprinkle with cheese. Makes 4 servings.

Bavarian Wiener Bake

1 pound (8 to 10) frankfurters
1 can condensed cream of
  mushroom soup
½ cup mayonnaise
1 teaspoon caraway seed
1 1-pound can (2 cups)
  sauerkraut, drained
4 cups diced cooked potatoes
½ cup buttered soft bread crumbs
¼ teaspoon paprika

Halve 4 franks; reserve. Slice remaining franks ¼ inch thick. Mix soup and mayonnaise. Combine sliced franks with *half* of soup mixture, the caraway seed, and kraut; spread in an 11½x7½x1½-inch baking dish. Stir remaining soup mixture into potatoes; arrange around edge of dish.

Combine buttered crumbs and paprika; sprinkle over potatoes. Arrange halved franks in design on top of casserole. Bake in moderate oven (350°) 30 minutes or till hot. Makes 5 or 6 servings.

Ham-Potato Soup

Combine 1 can frozen condensed cream of potato soup, 1 can condensed cream of mushroom soup, and 2 soup cans milk. Stir in one 2¼-ounce can deviled ham. Heat just to boiling. Makes 4 or 5 servings.

Skillet Beans 'n Franks

Sure to win kid approval—and ready to serve in 5 to 10 minutes—

2 tablespoons butter or margarine
1 cup diced tomato
½ teaspoon crushed oregano
¼ teaspoon garlic powder
2 1-pound cans (4 cups) beans
    and franks in tomato sauce

In skillet, melt butter; add tomato, oregano, and garlic powder; cook a minute to blend flavors; add beans and franks.

Heat, stirring often, till mixture is piping hot. Makes 6 servings.

Bean Banquet

2 1-pound cans (4 cups) pork
    and beans in tomato sauce
¼ cup catsup
2 tablespoons prepared mustard
1 teaspoon Worcestershire sauce
1 to 1½ teaspoons liquid smoke
• • •
2 12-ounce cans luncheon meat

In a 10x6x1½-inch baking dish, combine beans, catsup, and seasonings.

Cut meat in half lengthwise. *Cutting not quite through,* slice each half in 7 crosswise slices. Arrange meat "accordions" on beans. Bake in moderate oven (375°) 25 to 30 minutes, or till beans are bubbling hot. Place in broiler a few minutes to brown meat; brush meat with melted butter. Makes 6 to 8 servings.

Bologna Bake

¾ pound big Bologna, diced (2 cups)
1 cup celery slices
¼ cup sliced stuffed olives
4 hard-cooked eggs, diced
¼ cup chopped onion
1 tablespoon prepared mustard
Dash pepper
¾ cup mayonnaise
• • •
1 cup crushed potato chips

Combine all ingredients except potato chips. Place in 8¼x1¾-inch round ovenware cake dish; sprinkle with crushed potato chips. Bake in hot oven (400°) 20 to 25 minutes. Makes 4 or 5 servings.

Sausage-Noodle Treat

1 package brown-and-serve
    sausage links
• • •
1 package chicken-noodle dinner
1 8-ounce can (1 cup) tomatoes
2 tablespoons instant minced onion
2 teaspoons parsley flakes

Halve sausage links and brown in skillet according to label directions. Following directions for packaged dinner, add sauce mix, and cook. Meanwhile cook noodles as directed; drain, then add to skillet along with remaining ingredients. Heat thoroughly. Makes 5 servings.

Soup-kettle Supper

Three soups make a grand new full-meal soup. Serve with crackers and crisp celery sticks. And plan a luscious dessert—

1 can condensed cream of
    vegetable soup
1 can condensed cream of
    chicken soup
1 can condensed onion soup
1½ cups milk
1 12-ounce can (1½ cups) whole
    kernel corn
• • •
1 4-ounce can Vienna sausage

Mix soups together; stir in milk and corn. Slice sausage links in coins; add. Cover; heat slowly, stirring often till soup comes just to boiling. Makes 6 servings.

Chicken Livers Stroganoff

2 cups thinly sliced onion
¼ cup butter or margarine
½ pound chicken livers, halved
1 tablespoon paprika
½ teaspoon salt
Dash pepper
1 cup dairy sour cream
Hot cooked rice

Cook onion in butter till tender but not brown. Add chicken livers. Season with paprika, salt, and pepper. Slowly brown livers. Cover and cook over low heat 10 minutes or till livers are tender.

Add sour cream; heat through. Serve over hot cooked rice. Garnish with parsley, if desired. Makes 4 servings.

Oriental Quick Chick

1 10½-ounce can chicken a la king
1 5-ounce can (⅔ cup)
  chicken, diced
¼ cup light cream
1 to 2 tablespoons chopped
  candied ginger
¼ cup slivered blanched
  almonds, toasted
Hot fluffy rice

In saucepan, combine first 4 ingredients. Simmer uncovered 5 minutes, stirring occasionally. Add toasted almonds. Serve over hot fluffy rice. Makes 4 servings.

Chicken Pot Pie

2 1-pound cans (4 cups) chicken
  in gravy
⅓ cup milk
1 cup packaged biscuit mix
Paprika

Place chicken in gravy in wide 3-quart saucepan (to make room for dumplings). Heat till bubbling.

Add milk to biscuit mix, and prepare and cook dumplings according to package directions. Before serving, sprinkle with paprika. Makes 6 servings.

Cheese-Chicken Divine

1 10½-ounce can chicken a la king
1 can condensed cream of celery soup
¾ cup shredded sharp process
  American cheese
1 teaspoon prepared mustard
½ teaspoon Worcestershire sauce
½ teaspoon curry powder

· · ·

2 cups fine noodles
1 10-ounce package frozen
  broccoli spears

Heat chicken, soup, cheese, and seasonings till cheese melts, stirring frequently.

Meanwhile cook noodles in boiling *unsalted* water till tender; cook broccoli in boiling salted water till just tender. Drain noodles and broccoli.

Place noodles in greased 10x6x1½-inch baking dish. Arrange broccoli atop; pour chicken mixture over. Bake in moderate oven (375°) 10 to 15 minutes. Serves 4.

Eggs a la King

1 cup chopped celery
¼ cup chopped green pepper
¼ cup finely chopped onion
1 can condensed cream of celery soup
½ cup milk
1 cup diced process American cheese
4 hard-cooked eggs, chopped
6 stuffed green olives, sliced

Cook vegetables in 2 tablespoons hot fat till tender. Add soup, milk, and cheese; heat and stir till cheese melts. Add eggs and olives; heat through. Spoon over toast. Makes 4 servings.

Bacon-Hominy Scramble

Cook 4 slices bacon till crisp; drain, reserving 2 tablespoons drippings. Lightly brown one No. 2 can (2½ cups) hominy in reserved drippings.

Beat together 4 eggs, ½ teaspoon salt, and a dash pepper. Add to hominy. Cook till eggs are just set, stirring frequently. Season. Crumble bacon atop. Serves 6.

Easy Lobster Rabbit

2 9-ounce cans (2 cups) Welsh rabbit
1 5- or 6-ounce can (1 cup) lobster,
  drained and cubed
1 3-ounce can broiled sliced
  mushrooms
2 tablespoons cooking sauterne

Heat and stir rabbit over low heat just till simmering. Add lobster and drained mushrooms. Heat through. Add sauterne and spoon over hot toast points. Serves 4.

Speedy Shrimp Skillet

Place 1 can frozen condensed cream of shrimp soup in skillet; pour ¾ cup boiling water over. Cover; bring just to boil.

Stir in ⅔ cup packaged precooked rice, one 7-ounce package frozen cleaned shrimp, and ½ cup *each* diced celery and diced green pepper. Season with ½ teaspoon salt and dash pepper.

Cover, bring to boiling; reduce heat and simmer 10 minutes or till rice and shrimp are done; stir occasionally.

At serving time, add ½ cup sliced ripe olives; sprinkle with grated Parmesan.

Makes 4 servings.

Tuna Jackstraw Casserole

When time's a-flying and the family is "starving," a can opener is your best friend! This casserole is as delicious as it is quick—it's bound to be a favorite!

Tuna Jackstraw Casserole

1 4-ounce can shoestring potatoes

* * *

1 can condensed cream of
  mushroom soup
1 6½-, 7-, or 9¼-ounce can
  tuna, drained
1 6-ounce can (⅔ cup) evaporated milk
1 3-ounce can (⅔ cup) broiled
  sliced mushrooms, drained
¼ cup chopped pimiento

Reserve 1 cup of shoestring potatoes for topper. Combine remaining potatoes with the other ingredients. Pour into 1½-quart casserole. Arrange reserved potatoes on top. Bake uncovered in moderate oven (375°) 20 to 25 minutes or until thoroughly heated. Makes 4 to 6 servings.

Cheese-y Fish Sticks

Place frozen breaded fish sticks on baking sheet. Sprinkle with shredded Parmesan. Bake fish sticks, according to the package directions.

Friday Franks

¼ cup butter or margarine, melted
2 tablespoons lemon juice
1 8-ounce package frozen breaded
  fish sticks
5 split toasted coney buns
Sandwich spread

Mix butter and lemon juice. Dip fish sticks, coating all sides. Bake at 450° about 12 minutes. Spread buns generously with sandwich spread; place 2 fish sticks in each. Pass catsup, thin onion slices and cucumber slices. Makes 5 servings.

Hurry Tuna Curry

Cook ⅓ cup chopped onion, ¼ cup chopped green pepper, and 1 clove garlic, minced, in 2 tablespoons butter or margarine till tender but not brown. Stir in 1 cup dairy sour cream, 1 teaspoon curry powder, ¼ teaspoon salt, and dash pepper.

Break one 6½-, 7-, or 9¼-ounce can tuna in bite-size pieces; add. Heat slowly, stirring often. Serve over rice. Serves 4.

Tops! Garden Salad Buffet plus a flavorful bread

It's a flavor parade—chilled cooked broccoli spears and halved hard-cooked eggs rate a topper of luscious low-cal Yogurt Curry Sauce. Herbed Tomatoes have marinated to well-seasoned goodness. For color *and* flavor accent—slivery lemon slices, glossy ripe olives.

Salad partner is tempting Onion-Cheese Bread. The browned, crinkly look is from dots of butter and cheese melting atop as it bakes.

Skip-a-step salads

Garden Salad Buffet

Line chilled platter with frilly lettuce leaves. Arrange chilled cooked broccoli spears with paper-thin lemon slices, halved hard-cooked eggs, Herbed Tomatoes, and ripe olives. Pass Yogurt Curry Sauce.

Herbed Tomatoes

6 large ripe tomatoes
• • •
1 teaspoon salt
¼ teaspoon coarse black pepper
Few leaves fresh thyme or
    marjoram or ½ teaspoon of dried
¼ cup finely snipped parsley
¼ cup snipped chives
⅔ cup salad oil
¼ cup tarragon vinegar

Peel tomatoes; cut crosswise in half. Place in deep bowl, sprinkling each layer with seasonings and herbs. Combine oil and vinegar and pour over, tilting bowl so all tomatoes are coated.

Cover; chill an hour or so, occasionally spooning dressing over tomatoes. Drain off dressing to pass in bowl, if desired; arrange tomato halves on platter. Serves 6.

Yogurt Curry Sauce

Combine 1 cup yogurt, 1 tablespoon prepared mustard, 1 teaspoon seasoned salt, and ½ to 1 teaspoon curry powder. Snip parsley atop. Chill. Makes 1 cup.

Calico Vegetable Molds

Dissolve one 3-ounce package lemon-flavored gelatin in 1¾ cups boiling water. Add 2 tablespoons vinegar and ¼ teaspoon salt. Chill till partially set.

Add ½ cup cooked drained sliced or diced carrots, ½ cup drained cooked or canned peas, ¼ cup radish slices, and 3 tablespoons sliced green onion

Pour into individual molds. Chill firm. Unmold on greens. Makes 4 to 6 servings.

A-B-C Tomato Aspic

1 3-ounce package lemon-
    flavored gelatin
1¼ cups boiling water
1 8-ounce can (1 cup) seasoned
    tomato sauce
1 tablespoon vinegar
½ teaspoon seasoned salt
Salt and fresh-ground pepper to taste

Dissolve gelatin in boiling water; add remaining ingredients. Pour into individual molds. Chill firm. Unmold. Serves 4.

Jellied Cranberry Relish

1 3-ounce package strawberry-
    flavored gelatin
1 cup boiling water
1 9-ounce can (1 cup) pineapple
    tidbits
1 10-ounce package frozen
    cranberry relish, thawed
⅓ cup diced celery

Dissolve gelatin in boiling water. Drain pineapple, reserving syrup. Add water to syrup to make ¾ cup; add to gelatin along with relish. Chill till partially set. Stir in pineapple and celery. Pour into 1-quart mold; chill till firm. Makes 6 servings.

Easy-does-it Fruit Mold

2 cups pineapple-grapefruit-
    juice drink
1 3-ounce package lemon-flavored
    gelatin
1 No. 2½ can (3½ cups) fruit
    cocktail, well drained

Heat *1 cup* of the juice drink to boiling; add gelatin and stir until dissolved. Add remaining juice drink. Chill till partially set. Stir in fruit cocktail. Pour into 1-quart mold. Chill until firm. Unmold on salad greens. Serves 6.

Pass *Horseradish Dressing:* Blend 1 cup dairy sour cream, 1 tablespoon prepared horseradish, and ½ teaspoon salt.

Triple Bean Toss

1 1-pound can cut green beans
1 1-pound can (2 cups) cut wax beans
1 1-pound can (2 cups) kidney beans
2 tablespoons chopped green onions
¾ cup Italian salad dressing

Drain all beans. Add remaining ingredients to beans and toss to mix; season to taste with salt. Refrigerate several hours or overnight. Before serving, toss again, then drain. Dash with fresh-ground pepper. Serve on lettuce. Makes 10 servings.

Mexican Bean Salad: Follow above recipe, substituting one 1-pound can chick peas for wax beans, and omitting onions. Marinate in garlic French dressing. Serve on lettuce. Sprinkle with pickle relish.

Men's Favorite Tossed Salad

1 3½-ounce can French-fried onions
½ medium head lettuce
5 cups fresh spinach (stems removed)
⅓ cup Italian dressing

Heat onions in moderate oven a few minutes to crisp. Break lettuce and spinach in bite-size pieces. Scatter warm onions atop. Add dressing; toss lightly. Serves 6.

1-2-3 Relish

Combine ½ cup chopped green pepper, ½ cup chopped onion, and ½ cup chili sauce. If desired, chill. Makes 1¼ cups.

Easy Corn Relish

1 tablespoon cornstarch
¼ cup water
• • •
1 12-ounce can (1½ cups) Mexican-style whole-kernel corn, undrained
⅓ cup sugar
⅓ cup vinegar
1 teaspoon turmeric
1 teaspoon instant minced onion
½ teaspoon celery seed

Blend cornstarch and water in sauce pan; add remaining ingredients. Cook and stir over medium heat till mixture thickens and boils. Chill. Makes 2 cups.

Cottage Cheese Relish

¾ cup dairy sour cream
1½ cups large-curd cream-style cottage cheese, well-drained
¼ cup diced green peppers
¼ cup sliced green onion
2 tablespoons chopped pimiento
¼ teaspoon salt
Dash pepper

Blend sour cream with cottage cheese. Stir in chilled vegetables, salt, and pepper. Serve on lettuce. Team with tomato and green-pepper slices and olives on relish tray. Or serve in tomato cups. Serves 4.

Parmesan Blue-cheese Dressing

2 cups mayonnaise or salad dressing
1 8-ounce can seasoned tomato sauce
¼ cup grated Parmesan cheese
1 ounce blue cheese, crumbled (¼ cup)
2 tablespoons cooking sherry
2 cloves garlic, minced
1 teaspoon paprika

Mix all ingredients. (For a smooth dressing, whiz in blender for 10 to 15 seconds.) Chill. Serve over lettuce and tomatoes. Makes about 3½ cups.

Gourmet Dressing

3 tablespoons vinegar
1 envelope French salad-dressing mix
2 tablespoons salad oil
⅔ cup tomato juice

Pour vinegar into cruet; add salad-dressing mix and shake well. Add salad oil and tomato juice. Shake. Makes 1 cup.

Chili Mayonnaise

Stir ½ cup chili sauce into 1 cup mayonnaise. Makes 1½ cups dressing.

Lemon Mayonnaise

½ cup mayonnaise or salad dressing
¼ cup frozen lemonade concentrate
½ cup whipping cream, whipped

Blend mayonnaise and concentrate. Fold in whipped cream. Makes 1½ cups.

Vegetable quicks

Cottage Mashed Potatoes

    Instant mashed or whipped potatoes
       (enough for 4 servings)
    1½ tablespoons instant minced onion
    1 cup large-curd cream-style
       cottage cheese

Decreasing water by ½ cup, prepare instant potatoes according to package directions, *but adding instant onion to boiling water before adding potatoes*. With fork, fold in cheese. Turn into 1-quart casserole. Dot with butter; sprinkle with paprika. Bake at 350° 30 minutes. Makes 4 or 5 servings.

Lightning Creamed Potatoes

    ⅓ cup water
    1½ teaspoons salt
    4 cups pared potatoes, cut in
       bite-size pieces
    ⅓ cup finely chopped onion
    ½ cup light cream

In pressure pan, combine water, salt, potatoes, and onion. Cover; bring to 15 pounds pressure. *Immediately* remove from heat and let pressure go down *normally*. Add cream. Snip parsley over. Serves 6.

Crunch-top Potatoes

    ⅓ cup butter or margarine
    3 or 4 large baking potatoes, pared,
       cut in ½-inch crosswise slices
    ¾ cup crushed corn flakes
    1½ cups shredded sharp cheese
    2 teaspoons salt
    1½ teaspoons paprika

Melt butter in 15½x10½x1-inch pan at 375°. Add single layer of potatoes; turn once in butter. Mix remaining ingredients; sprinkle over. Bake ½ hour or till done and tops are crisp. Serve hot.

Hawaiian Rice

    1⅓ cups packaged precooked rice
    ⅓ to ½ cup flaked coconut

Prepare rice according to package directions; add coconut; toss to mix. Makes 3 cups. Serve with curry or sweet-sour pork.

Skillet Hominy in Sour Cream

    2 cans hominy
    2 tablespoons butter
    1 cup dairy sour cream

Drain hominy; put in skillet with butter. Cover with sour cream. Heat on low heat, stirring often, till cooked down. Season to taste. Makes 8 servings.

Gourmet Onions

Slice 5 medium onions; season with ½ teaspoon *each* monosodium glutamate, sugar, salt, and pepper. Cook in ⅓ cup butter 5 to 8 minutes or till barely tender, stirring to separate rings. Add ½ cup cooking sherry; cook quickly 2 or 3 minutes. Sprinkle with 2 tablespoons shredded Parmesan cheese. Makes 6 servings.

Easy elegance, Gourmet Onions

Corn Curry

A new way with corn — it's delicious—

   3 tablespoons butter
   1½ to 2 cups cut fresh or frozen corn*
   2 tablespoons chopped green pepper
   2 tablespoons chopped onion
   ¼ to ½ teaspoon curry powder
      • • •
   ½ cup dairy sour cream
   Salt and pepper

Melt butter in skillet. Add vegetables and curry. Cover; cook over low heat till vegetables are just tender, 8 to 10 minutes. Stir in sour cream; season to taste. Heat, stirring constantly. Makes 4 servings.

   *Or, use drained canned whole-kernel corn, or leftover corn cut off the cob; add with the sour cream.

Zucchini Parmesan

Cook just till tender; toss with zesty cheese—

   4 or 5 small zucchini squash, thinly
     sliced (about 3 cups)
   2 tablespoons butter or margarine
   ½ teaspoon salt
   Dash pepper
   2 tablespoons grated Parmesan cheese

Put zucchini, butter, and seasonings in skillet. Cover; cook slowly 5 minutes. Uncover; cook, turning slices, till barely tender, about 5 minutes more. Sprinkle with cheese; toss. Makes 4 servings.

Kidney-bean Casserole

Include this in an oven-going meal—

   2 1-pound cans (4 cups) kidney beans
   8 slices bacon
   ½ cup chopped onion
   ⅓ cup chili sauce
   Salt and pepper

Drain beans, reserving 3 tablespoons liquid. Cook bacon till crisp; drain, reserving 2 tablespoons drippings. Crumble bacon. Cook onion in reserved bacon drippings till tender but not brown. Add beans, reserved liquid, bacon, chili sauce, seasonings. Pour into ungreased 1-quart casserole. Cover; bake at 350° 20 minutes or till heated through. Makes 4 to 6 servings.

Speedy Ways with Peas

• Add chopped mint to peas while cooking.
• Add nutmeg and chopped pickled onions to hot cooked peas just before serving.
• Drop in savory or thyme while cooking.

Green Beans, Cream Style

   1 10-ounce package frozen green beans
   1 3-ounce package cream
     cheese, softened
   1 tablespoon milk
   ¾ teaspoon celery seed
   ¼ teaspoon salt

Cook beans according to package directions; drain. Combine remaining ingredients; blend thoroughly. Spoon over *hot* beans. Makes 4 servings.

Baby Beets in Sour Cream

   ¼ cup dairy sour cream
   1 tablespoon vinegar
   1 teaspoon minced green onion
   ¾ teaspoon sugar
   ½ teaspoon salt
   Dash cayenne
   2½ cups halved cooked beets, drained

Combine ingredients, except beets; mix well. Add sauce to beets; heat slowly, stirring to coat. Serves 4 or 5.

3-Minute Hollandaise

   ¼ cup mayonnaise or salad dressing
   ¼ cup dairy sour cream
   ½ teaspoon prepared mustard
   1 teaspoon lemon juice

Combine ingredients. Heat over low heat. Serve with broccoli. Makes ½ cup.

Swiss Cheese Sauce

   ½ cup shredded process Swiss cheese
   ¼ cup mayonnaise or salad dressing
   ½ cup dairy sour cream

Combine cheese and mayonnaise. Cook over low heat, stirring constantly, till cheese melts. (If necessary, beat smooth with rotary beater.) Mix in sour cream; heat. Dash with paprika. Serve with hot cauliflower or asparagus. Makes 1 cup.

Hurry-up hot breads

Onion-Cheese Supper Bread

½ cup chopped onion
1 beaten egg
½ cup milk
1½ cups packaged biscuit mix
1 cup shredded sharp process
   American cheese
2 tablespoons snipped parsley
2 tablespoons melted butter

Cook onion in small amount hot fat till tender but not brown. Combine egg and milk; add to biscuit mix; stir only till mix is just moistened. Add onion, *half* the cheese, and parsley. Spread dough in greased 8x1½-inch round cake pan. Sprinkle with remaining cheese. Drizzle melted butter over. Bake at 400° 20 minutes or till toothpick comes out clean. Makes 6 to 8 servings. Perfect salad go-with. See page 14.

Bacon Bars

½ cup shredded sharp process
   American cheese
6 slices bacon, crisp-cooked and
   coarsely crumbled
2 cups packaged biscuit mix
3 tablespoons bacon drippings

Stir cheese and bacon into dry mix. Make dough according to package directions for rich biscuits, substituting bacon drippings for salad oil. Knead as directed for rolled biscuits. Roll to 10x6 inches. Cut in six 10-inch strips, 1-inch wide; cut each in thirds crosswise, to make 18 bars. Place 1 inch apart on ungreased baking sheet. Bake at 450° 10 minutes. Makes 18.

Double Corn Muffins

Prepare 1 package corn-muffin mix. Stir in one 1-pound can whole kernel corn, drained. Spoon into greased muffin pans, filling ⅔ full. Drop spoonful deviled ham (takes one 2¼-ounce can) on each muffin. Bake at 375° for 20 minutes. Makes 12.

Herb Rolls

Pan rolls just like Grandma's—

1 package active dry yeast
¾ cup warm water
2½ cups packaged biscuit mix
½ teaspoon celery seed
1 teaspoon poultry seasoning

Soften yeast in *warm* water. Stir in biscuit mix and remaining ingredients; beat vigorously (2 to 3 minutes). Turn out on surface well-dusted with biscuit mix. Knead till smooth, about 25 strokes. Roll in a 14x6-inch rectangle, about ¼ inch thick. Cut dough lengthwise in thirds, then crosswise at 2-inch intervals to make 21 squares. Form each in ball.

In greased 8x1½-inch round pan, arrange 13 rolls (not quite touching each other) around edge; arrange an inner circle of 8 rolls, leaving a 2-inch hole in center. Cover with damp cloth. Let rise in warm place till double (about 1 hour). Bake in a hot oven (400°) 15 to 20 minutes or till golden brown. Serve hot. Makes 21.

Topper Corn Bread

Rich cheese topping bakes down in to dimple corn bread! Try this with fried chicken—

¼ cup chopped onion
1 tablespoon butter or margarine
1 package corn-muffin mix or
   corn-bread mix
1 cup shredded sharp process
   American cheese
1 teaspoon celery seed

Cook onion in butter till tender but not brown. Prepare mix according to package directions; spread batter in a greased 10x 6x1½-inch baking dish. Sprinkle cheese evenly over batter; dot onion-butter mixture over all; sprinkle with celery seed. Bake in moderate oven (375°) about 20 minutes or till done. Serve at once.

Little Orange Loaves

Orange-muffin mix turns into nut bread—

1 package orange-muffin mix
¾ cup canned whole cranberry sauce
1 cup chopped California walnuts

Prepare batter from muffin mix according to package directions. Stir in cranberry sauce and nuts. Spoon into six greased 6-ounce frozen-juice-concentrate cans.

Bake in moderate oven (375°) 30 to 35 minutes or till done. Cool 5 minutes; ease out of cans with spatula (cut end out of can). Bread slices best second day.

Marmalade Bread

1 loaf French bread (about
   12 inches long)
        • • •
⅓ to ½ cup soft butter or
   margarine
½ cup orange marmalade
Cinnamon

Cut bread in 1- to 1½-inch diagonal slices. Spread with butter, then with marmalade (don't skimp!). Sprinkle cinnamon generously over top. Place slices, marmalade side up, on ungreased baking sheet. Heat in hot oven (400°)* about 8 minutes, or till hot. Makes 8 to 10 slices.

*Or place on broiler rack and broil 5 to 6 inches from heat 6 to 7 minutes. Remember, marmalade topping will be *extra hot*, so let cool a few minutes before serving.

Toasted Marmalade Bread

Cooky-crumb Coffeecake

Crumbled cookies make a different "fun" topper—

2 cups packaged biscuit mix
⅓ cup sugar
2 tablespoons soft butter or
   margarine
2 eggs
⅔ cup milk
2 teaspoons vanilla
1 cup fine vanilla-sandwich-cooky
   crumbs (9 cookies)
⅓ cup sugar
½ cup broken California walnuts
3 tablespoons butter, melted

Combine first 6 ingredients. Beat at medium speed 2 minutes, scraping sides of bowl often. Turn half the batter into a greased 10x6x1¾-inch baking dish. Combine last 4 ingredients; mix till crumbly. Reserve ½ cup mixture for topping; sprinkle remainder over batter in pan. Spoon remaining batter over; add reserved topping. Bake at 350° 30 minutes or till done.

Spicy Coffee Ring

Perfect California walnut halves
1 package refrigerated biscuits
Melted butter or margarine
⅓ cup brown sugar
1 teaspoon cinnamon
2 tablespoons seedless raisins

Place ring of walnut halves in greased 5½-cup ring mold, Dip biscuits in melted butter, then in mixture of brown sugar and cinnamon. Place in mold, overlapping slightly. Tuck raisins between biscuits. Bake at 425° 13 to 15 minutes.

Toasty Cheese Loaf (*See cover*)

1 loaf French bread (12 inches long)
⅓ cup butter or margarine
1 5-ounce jar sharp spreading cheese

Cut loaf in half lengthwise horizontally. Cut each half in 2-inch diagonal slices, cutting to, but not through, bottom crust. Place on baking sheet. Blend butter and cheese. Spread between slices and over top. Bake in hot oven (400°) till cheese is melty and bread is crusty, about 15 minutes. Serve immediately. Serves 10.

Tangy fix-up— Parsley Fantans

Melt 2 tablespoons butter; add 1 teaspoon lemon juice. Combine 2 tablespoons *each* chopped parsley and chopped chives. Partially separate sections of 6 brown-and-serve butterflake rolls. Brush sections with part of butter; sprinkle with part of parsley-chive mixture. Place in muffin cups. Brush tops with remaining butter; sprinkle with parsley and chives. Brown at 400° about 10 minutes.

Parmesan Slices

Crusty and delicious, each slice is covered with golden cheese and poppy seed—

    ¼ cup butter or margarine, melted
    ½ cup grated Parmesan cheese
    6 1-inch slices French or Vienna bread
    1 tablespoon poppy seed (optional)

Combine butter, cheese; spread on both sides of each bread slice. Sprinkle both sides with poppy seed. Place on baking sheet; toast at 350° 12 minutes, turn once.

Garlic-bread Sticks

    1 unsliced sandwich loaf (11-inch)
    ½ cup butter or margarine, melted
    2 cloves garlic, minced
    ¼ cup sesame seed, toasted

Trim crusts. Cut loaf in half crosswise, then in half lengthwise. Cut each piece crosswise in 4 sticks, 1¼ inches thick. Combine butter and garlic; brush on all sides of sticks; sprinkle with sesame seed. Arrange in 13x9x2-inch baking dish (not touching each other). Toast in hot oven (400°) about 10 minutes. Makes about 16 sticks.

Onion Biscuits

Hot biscuits with wonderful onion flavor to enhance a supper of cold cuts and salad—

    2 tablespoons instant minced onion
    2 tablespoons butter or
      margarine, melted
    1 package refrigerated biscuits

Add onion to butter; let stand few minutes. Place biscuits on ungreased baking sheet. Press a hollow in center of each biscuit with floured bottom of small glass. Fill hollows with butter mixture. Bake at 450° 8 to 10 minutes or till done. Makes 10.

Onion Slices

    1 loaf French bread (18-inch)
    ½ cup chopped green onions and tops
    ½ cup soft butter or margarine

Cut bread in half horizontally. Combine onions and butter; spread on cut sides of bread. Then slash each half loaf on the bias in 1½- to 2-inch slices, *but don't cut quite through bottom crust*. Place on baking sheet and heat in hot oven (400°) 10 minutes or till toasty and golden brown.

Dandy do-little desserts

Butterscotch Torte Supreme

Call on 3 mixes, add dates and nuts; presto, you create the sky-high beauty shown on page 4 —

1 package yellow-cake mix

. . .

1 4-ounce package butterscotch pudding
1 8-ounce package pitted dates, cut up (1¼ cups)
Dash salt
½ cup chopped California walnuts
2 tablespoons butter or margarine

. . .

1 package fluffy white frosting mix

Prepare cake mix according to package directions; bake in two 9-inch round cake pans. Cool thoroughly.

Meanwhile, prepare pudding according to directions, *but using only 1½ cups milk and adding dates and salt.* When done, remove from heat; add nuts and butter. Cover surface closely with clear plastic wrap or waxed paper; cool to room temperature.

Cut each cake layer in half, using thread. Fill between layers and spread over top.

Prepare frosting mix according to package directions. Spread on sides and add 1½-inch border of frosting on top of cake. Store any leftover cake in the refrigerator.

Angel Cake with Coffee Cream

1 package angel-cake mix*

. . .

2 cups whipping cream
½ cup sugar
1½ tablespoons instant coffee
1 teaspoon vanilla

Prepare and bake angel cake according to package directions. Cool thoroughly. Whip cream with the sugar, coffee, and vanilla till mixture will hold in peaks. Frost top and sides of cake. Garnish with chocolate shot or toasted almonds.

*Or buy a 10-inch tube angel cake at the baked goods counter.

Almond Flip-top Cake

It's an upside-down surprise! —

2 teaspoons butter or margarine
1 tablespoon sugar
⅛ cup chopped or ready-diced almonds

. . .

1 loaf-size white or yellow cake mix*

. . .

1 recipe Orange Filling

Melt butter in an 8x8x2-inch pan; spread over bottom and sprinkle with sugar, then with almonds. Prepare cake mix according to package directions. Carefully pour the batter over the nuts.

Bake in moderate oven (375°) 25 to 30 minutes. Invert on rack and cool. Split cake into 2 layers; spread cooled Orange Filling between. Makes 9 squares.

*Or prepare 2-layer cake mix and use *half;* bake remainder as cupcakes.

Orange Filling

Fresh flavor. Delicious cake complement —

½ cup sugar
3 tablespoons all-purpose flour
Dash salt
½ cup orange juice

. . .

1 beaten egg

. . .

1 tablespoon butter or margarine
2 teaspoons lemon juice
2 teaspoons grated orange peel

Thoroughly mix together sugar, flour, and salt. Stir in orange juice. Cook over low heat, stirring constantly, until mixture thickens and becomes clear.

Stir small amount of hot mixture into beaten egg, then stir into remaining hot mixture. Cook and stir over low heat 3 to 4 minutes longer. Blend in butter, lemon juice, and orange peel; cool the mixture thoroughly. Makes ¾ cup filling.

Petite cakes—just the ticket to
refreshment on hot summer evenings.
Baby Orange Babas play a double
role—serve while still warm in winter!

Baby Orange Babas

1 package yellow-cake mix

. . .

¾ cup sugar
¾ cup water
¾ cup orange juice
3 tablespoons orange peel, cut in
thin slivers (white part removed)

Prepare the batter from cake mix according to the package directions. Place *well-
greased* paper hot-drink cups on a baking
sheet, and spoon in the batter, filling the
cups about half full.

Bake in moderate oven (375°) 25 minutes
or till done (test with cake tester).

Meanwhile, make syrup: Combine sugar, water, orange juice and orange peel;
cook mixture for 5 minutes.

When cakes are done, cool a minute or
two, then turn out of cups onto serving
plate. Drizzle immediately with hot orange
syrup, soaking the cakes well. Chill. Serve
cold with whipped cream. Makes 9 or 10.

Chocolate-Mint Shortcakes

*Easy as making toast. Another time, vary the
flavors of ice cream and syrup—*

Cut 4 slices of loaf pound cake. Toast
the slices (for easy removal from the con-
ventional toaster, put cake slices in with
the narrow end down).

Place a slice of toasted cake on each dessert plate and top each with a scoop of
peppermint ice cream. Pour canned chocolate syrup over all. Makes 4 servings.

Coconut Cake Bars

*These warm "cake-cookies" boast a chewy
coconut-honey "frosting"—*

Slice a pound cake ½ inch thick. Cut
each slice into 4 strips. Spread three sides
with butter and honey; roll in flaked coconut; place on greased cooky sheet. Toast
in moderate oven (375°) about 5 to 10
minutes or till delicate brown.

Delightful party duet—
Easy Macaroons (page 27)
and sparkly Cranberry
Danish Cream rate praises galore!

Berries in Custard Sauce

1 3⅝- or 3¾-ounce package
  instant vanilla pudding
½ teaspoon vanilla
1 pint fresh strawberries

Prepare pudding according to package directions, *but using 2½ cups milk and adding vanilla*. Chill about 30 minutes or until mixture is the consistency of custard sauce. (If mixture gets too firm, beat with rotary beater till smooth.)

Cut any large strawberries in half; sugar all lightly. Pile berries in dessert dishes and spoon the custard sauce over. Makes 4 or 5 servings. Top with whole berries.

Cranberry Danish Cream

1 package currant-raspberry-
  flavored Danish dessert
1 pint bottle cranberry-juice cocktail
1 package custard-flavored dessert mix
½ cup whipping cream, whipped
Slivered blanched almonds, toasted

Prepare Danish dessert according to directions, *but using cranberry-juice cocktail for the liquid*. Cool about 30 minutes.

Meanwhile prepare custard according to directions. Pour into sherbets and chill till set. Spoon Danish dessert *carefully* over custard; chill till set, about 3 hours. Top with fluffs of whipped cream and almonds. Serves 6 to 8.

Mocha Dessert

1 3- or 3¼-ounce package
  vanilla pudding
1 teaspoon vanilla
1 teaspoon instant coffee
½ cup semisweet chocolate pieces
Flaked coconut

Prepare pudding according to label directions and add vanilla. Divide in half. To one half, add the instant coffee and chocolate pieces; stir to dissolve.

Spoon the pudding into sherbets, alternating layers. Trim with coconut. Chill thoroughly. Makes 4 servings.

Double-chocolate Pudding

Fluffy and rich – designed for chocolate fans—

1 4-ounce package chocolate pudding
½ 6-ounce package (½ cup)
  semisweet chocolate pieces
1 teaspoon vanilla
1 cup whipping cream, whipped

Cook pudding according to package directions, *but adding ¼ cup more milk*. While mixture is hot, add semisweet chocolate pieces, stirring till melted. Cool. Add the vanilla and beat until the mixture is fluffy. Fold in whipped cream.

Spoon pudding into sherbets. Top with additional chocolate pieces. Chill thoroughly. Makes 6 to 8 servings.

Pineapple Dessert

A fluffy pudding flavored with the gentle tang of pineapple juice—

1 3- or 3¼-ounce package
  vanilla pudding
1 12-ounce can (1½ cups) unsweetened
  pineapple juice
    • • •
1 cup whipping cream, whipped
½ cup broken California walnuts
  (optional)

Prepare pudding according to the package directions, *but using 1½ cups pineapple juice instead of milk*. Cool thoroughly. Beat smooth; fold in whipped cream and nuts. Chill. Serve pudding topped with walnut halves. Makes 4 servings.

Peanut-butter Pudding

¼ cup peanut butter
2 cups milk
    • • •
1 4¼- or 4½-ounce package
  instant chocolate pudding

Beat peanut butter and ¼ *cup* milk with with rotary beater* till smooth. Slowly add remaining milk, beating until well blended. Add pudding mix; blend well, about 1 minute. Pour into serving dishes; chill.

*Or beat at lowest speed on mixer.

Apple-Nut Dessert

Smart cooking – bake this delicious pudding to round out an oven meal—

1 beaten egg
¾ cup sugar
½ teaspoon vanilla
    • • •
½ cup sifted all-purpose flour
1 teaspoon baking powder
¼ teaspoon salt
    • • •
1 cup chopped unpared tart apples
½ cup broken California walnuts

Combine egg, sugar, and vanilla. Sift together flour, baking powder, and salt. Add dry ingredients to egg mixture and blend well. Stir in apples and nuts. Spread in greased 8x8x2-inch baking dish.

Bake in moderate oven (350°) 30 minutes or till done. Cut in squares. Serve warm with ice cream. Makes 6 to 9 servings.

Baked Cherry Pudding

Golden-brown crumb top is cake mix—

1 No. 2 can (2½ cups) cherry-pie
  filling
1 package loaf-size yellow-cake mix
⅓ cup butter or margarine, melted

Spread pie filling in buttered 9x9x2-inch pan. Sprinkle cake mix evenly over top of filling; drizzle with butter.

Bake in moderate oven (350°) 40 to 45 minutes or till top is golden brown. Serve warm with ice cream. Makes 9 servings.

Chocolate Chiffon Dessert

    1 cup vanilla-wafer crumbs
    ¼ cup chopped walnuts
    3 tablespoons butter, melted
    1 envelope unflavored gelatin
    ¼ cup cold water
    ⅔ cup chocolate-flavored syrup
    ½ teaspoon vanilla
    1 cup evaporated milk, chilled
        icy cold

For crust, combine first 3 ingredients; press in 8x8x2-inch pan. Chill. Meanwhile, soften gelatin in cold water. Heat syrup; add gelatin; stir to dissolve. Cool to room temperature. Add vanilla. In chilled bowl, whip milk; fold in chocolate. Chill till mixture mounds *slightly* when spooned. Pour over crust. Chill firm. Serves 9.

Emerald Salad Dessert

    1 No. 2 can (2½ cups) pineapple tidbits
    1 3-ounce package lime-
        flavored gelatin
    2 cups tiny marshmallows
    1 2-ounce package dessert-
        topping mix

Drain pineapple, reserving syrup. Add water to syrup to make 2 cups; heat to boiling. Add gelatin; stir to dissolve. Add pineapple; pour into 10x6x1½-inch baking dish. Layer immediately with marshmallows. Prepare dessert-topping according to package directions. Spread over marshmallows. Chill firm. Cut in 8 to 10 squares.

Cherry Cheesecake Pie

    1 8-ounce package cream cheese,
        softened
    1 cup sifted confectioners' sugar
    1 teaspoon vanilla
    1 cup whipping cream, whipped
    ¼ teaspoon almond extract
    1 1-pound 6-ounce can
        cherry pie filling
    1 baked 9-inch pastry shell

Beat together cream cheese, sugar, and vanilla till smooth. Fold in whipped cream. Pour into pastry shell. Add almond extract to cherry pie filling and carefully spoon over cheese layer. Chill till set.

Summertime Apple Pie

    1 3-ounce package lemon-flavored
        gelatin
    1¾ cups boiling water
    1 No. 2 (2½ cups) can apple-pie filling
    ½ teaspoon cinnamon
    ¼ teaspoon nutmeg
    ½ teaspoon grated lemon peel
    1 9-inch graham-cracker crumb crust
    1 tablespoon sugar
    ½ cup shredded sharp American cheese
    ½ cup whipping cream, whipped

Dissolve gelatin in boiling water; chill till partially set. Combine pie filling, spices, peel. Reserve ¼ *cup* of the gelatin; stir remainder into apple mixture; pour into crust. For "meringue," fold reserved gelatin, the sugar, and cheese into whipped cream. Spread over pie; chill till firm.

Peach Petal Pie

    1 No. 2 can (2½ cups) peach-pie filling
    About 10 ¼-inch slices refrigerated
        slice-and-bake sugar cookies
    1 teaspoon sugar
    Dash cinnamon

Heat pie filling; pour into 8-inch pie plate. Overlap cooky slices around edge of pie plate. Mix sugar and cinnamon together; sprinkle over cookies. Bake in moderate oven (350°) 35 to 40 minutes or till cookies are done. Serve warm in sauce dishes with ice cream. Makes 5 servings.

Cranberry Cream Pie

    1 3-ounce package raspberry gelatin
    1¼ cups boiling water
    1 1-pound can whole cranberry sauce
    1 cup dairy sour cream
    1 9-inch baked pastry shell
    1¼ cups tiny marshmallows
    ½ cup whipping cream, whipped
    1 tablespoon sugar

Dissolve gelatin in boiling water; add the cranberry sauce. Chill till slightly thickened. Beat in sour cream with rotary beater till blended; chill till partially set. Spoon into pastry shell. Sprinkle marshmallows atop. Fold sugar into whipped cream, spread over pie. Chill till firm.

Strawberry-Angel Dessert

   1 3-ounce package strawberry-
     flavored gelatin
   1 cup boiling water
   2 10-ounce packages frozen straw-
     berries, partially thawed
   1 tablespoon lemon juice

        •   •

   1 3-ounce package lemon-chiffon
     pie filling
   8 cups 1-inch cubes angel cake*
   1 cup whipping cream, whipped

Dissolve the gelatin in water; add *1 package* strawberries and lemon juice. Chill till partially set. Prepare chiffon pie filling according to package directions. Fold into gelatin. Fold in cake cubes. Spread in a 13x9x2-inch baking dish. Chill till set.

    Cut in squares, garnish with whipped cream and remaining package of strawberries. Makes 12 to 15 servings.

    *Use a 10-inch tube cake. (You'll have a little cake left over to serve next day.)

Peanut Fudge Sauce

   1 cup chocolate syrup
   ½ cup chunk-style peanut butter

Stir chocolate syrup into peanut butter. Serve sauce over vanilla or chocolate ice cream. Pass crisp cookies.

Orange Sundae Sauce

   1 cup sugar
   ¼ cup water
   1 6-ounce can frozen orange-juice
     concentrate

Combine sugar and water in a small saucepan. Bring to a rolling boil, stirring constantly. Boil 1 minute. Remove from the heat; blend in juice concentrate. Cool; serve on vanilla ice cream. Makes 1½ cups.

Snow-on-the-Mountain Sundae

    Spoon marshmallow creme over chocolate ice cream. For easy "no-stick" serving: Place tablespoon in *hot* water for a few seconds before scooping marshmallow creme from jar. Fluffy marshmallow will slide right off the spoon—no sticking.

Easy Macaroons

Guests can't believe it—only 3 ingredients!—

   2 8-ounce packages shredded coconut
   1 15-ounce can (1⅓ cups)
     sweetened condensed milk
   2 teaspoons vanilla

Mix ingredients. Drop from teaspoon onto *well-greased* cooky sheet. Bake in moderate oven (350°) 8 minutes. Cool slightly; remove to rack. Makes 4½ to 5 dozen.

Speedy Ginger Cookies

   1 14-ounce package gingerbread mix
   ⅔ cup water
   ½ cup chunk-style peanut butter

      •   •   •

   ½ cup seedless raisins

Blend dry gingerbread mix with water and peanut butter. Beat vigorously ½ minute. Add raisins. Drop by heaping teaspoonfuls onto greased baking sheet. Bake in moderate oven (350°) 10 to 12 minutes or till done. Makes about 3 dozen cookies.

Chocolate Pudding Frosting

   1 4-ounce package chocolate pudding
   ¼ cup milk
   ¼ cup butter

      •   •   •

   1 teaspoon vanilla
   2 cups sifted confectioners' sugar
   1 tablespoon hot water

Combine pudding, milk and butter in saucepan. Bring mixture to boil over medium heat, stirring constantly, and boil 1 minute. Cool 15 minutes.

    Add vanilla and blend in confectioners' sugar. Add hot water. Mix well. Frosts top of one 13x9x2-inch cake.

Maple Butter Icing

   ⅓ cup soft butter
   3 cups sifted confectioners' sugar
   ½ cup maple syrup

Blend butter with sugar. Add syrup and beat mixture until well blended and fluffy. Frosts two 8-inch layers.

Big meals with

small appliances

Hot off the griddle

Grilled Crab Sandwiches

1 6½- or 7½-ounce can (about 1 cup)
crab meat, drained and flaked
½ cup shredded sharp process
American cheese
¼ cup chopped celery
2 tablespoons drained
sweet-pickle relish
2 tablespoons chopped green
onions and tops
1 hard-cooked egg, chopped
3 tablespoons salad dressing
½ teaspoon lemon juice
½ teaspoon prepared horseradish
• • •
10 slices bread, buttered generously
5 tomato slices

Combine first 9 ingredients; spread on *un-buttered* side of 5 bread slices. Add tomato slices; season with salt and pepper. Top with bread slices, buttered side up.

Grill on griddle or sandwich grill till sandwiches are golden brown. Makes 5.

Burgers in Bologna Boats

Each meat patty is cradled in a Bologna slice—great flavor combination. See picture, page 28—

1 pound ground beef
4 thin slices large Bologna
Salt and pepper
2 to 4 slices sharp process
American cheese, cut in strips
4 hamburger buns, split and toasted
Prepared mustard

Shape beef in 4 patties about same size around as Bologna slices. Grill on lightly greased griddle, turning once; sprinkle with salt and pepper. Slip each patty onto Bologna slice. Grill till Bologna is lightly browned and edges cup around patty.

Top with lattice of cheese strips. Spread bottom halves of toasted buns with mustard; top with patties; prop bun tops on edge to show off pretty lattice. Offer catsup, pickle relish, and burger relish. Serves 4.

Gourmet Steak on Toast

Sauce:
½ cup canned condensed beef broth
½ cup cooking claret
1 or 2 green onions, finely sliced
Dash *each* pepper, marjoram, and thyme
1 small bay leaf
¼ teaspoon lemon juice
1 teaspoon snipped parsley
2 teaspoons butter or margarine
• • •
4 cube steaks, ¼ inch thick
8 tomato wedges
4 ½-inch-wide green-pepper strips
4 bias-cut, ½-inch slices
French bread, toasted

Sauce: Combine broth, claret, onions, and seasonings; cook fast to reduce the volume by ½. Remove bay leaf; add lemon juice, parsley, and butter. (Set aside; keep hot.)

Grill cube steaks 1 to 2 minutes per side on lightly greased griddle. Meanwhile, grill green pepper and tomatoes alongside. Sprinkle all with salt and freshly ground pepper. To serve, dip toast quickly in Sauce; place a steak atop and arrange a green-pepper strip and 2 tomato wedges on steak. Spoon any remaining sauce over sandwiches. Makes 4 servings.

Fruit Grill

Drain canned pineapple slices, peach halves, or pear halves. Peel all-yellow bananas. Brush fruit liberally with melted butter or margarine. Sprinkle bananas with salt. Brown on electric griddle preheated to about 340°, turning once.

Sweet tooth? Sprinkle bananas with cinnamon sugar; fill centers of pears and peaches with currant jelly. Serve with hot sandwiches or grilled ham.

Appetizers on the griddle

Griddle can double as a hot tray for serving hot appetizers, like cracker canapes. Set temperature control at about 200°. Crackers stay crisp, toppings soft.

Grilled Steak Sandwich

1 pound ¼-inch-thick round steak
Instant meat tenderizer
½ cup butter, melted
3 tablespoons bottled steak sauce
2 tablespoons sliced green onion
1½ tablespoons Worcestershire sauce
¼ teaspoon salt
6 1-inch slices French bread

Cut steak in 6 pieces. Use tenderizer following directions. Preheat griddle to 400°; grease lightly. Grill meat 2 to 3 minutes per side. Pepper. Make sauce: Combine next 5 ingredients; heat. Toast bread. To serve, dip toast quickly in sauce; top with steak; spoon on remaining sauce. Serves 6.

Grilled Tomatoes

4 medium tomatoes
Salt and pepper
½ cup soft bread crumbs
¼ cup shredded sharp process
   American cheese
2 tablespoons butter or
   margarine, melted
2 tablespoons snipped parsley

Halve tomatoes (or cut in thick slices). Sprinkle cut surfaces with salt and freshly ground pepper. Mix bread crumbs, cheese, and butter; sprinkle over tomatoes. Trim with the snipped parsley.

Heat tomatoes, cut side up, on griddle about 5 minutes or until hot through.

Grilled Steak Sandwich   Dip thick slices of toasty French bread in savory sauce, crown with sizzling round steak. Serve with cheese-topped Grilled Tomatoes. Heat them on griddle alongside steak.

Easy fry-pan favorites

Hamburger Stroganoff

1 to 1½ pounds ground beef
3 slices bacon, diced
½ cup chopped onion
1½ tablespoons all-purpose flour
¾ teaspoon salt
¼ teaspoon paprika
Dash pepper
1 can condensed cream of mushroom
  soup
1 cup dairy sour cream
8 to 10 hamburger buns, split
  and toasted

Place ground beef and bacon in electric skillet, heat to about 350°. Cook and stir till beef is browned. Add onion and cook till just tender. Spoon off excess fat. Blend flour, seasonings into meat. Stir in soup. Cook, uncovered, at about 220° for 15 to 20 minutes, stirring often. Stir in sour cream; heat. Serve in buns. Serves 8 to 10.

Gourmet Goulash

1 pound ground beef
1 cup chopped onion
1 clove garlic, crushed
1 teaspoon salt
3 cups (4 ounces) medium noodles
1 No. 2 can (2½ cups) tomato juice
1½ teaspoons Worcestershire sauce
1½ teaspoons celery salt
1 teaspoon salt
Dash pepper
1 can condensed beef broth
½ cup water
⅓ cup chopped green pepper
1 cup dairy sour cream
1 3-ounce can (⅔ cup) broiled
  sliced mushrooms, drained

Place beef, onion, garlic, and 1 teaspoon salt in electric skillet. Heat to about 350°; cook and stir till beef is browned. Add noodles. Combine next 7 ingredients; pour over noodles. Cover; simmer at about 220° for 20 minutes, stirring occasionally. Add green pepper. Cover; cook 10 minutes or till noodles are tender. Stir in mushrooms, sour cream; heat. Serves 5 or 6.

Quick Spanish Rice

¼ cup shortening
½ cup chopped green pepper
½ cup chopped onion
1 12-ounce can luncheon meat, cut in
  thin strips
1 beef bouillon cube dissolved in
  1¼ cups boiling water
2 8-ounce cans seasoned tomato sauce
1 teaspoon sugar
Dash pepper
1⅓ cups packaged precooked rice

Preheat electric skillet to about 300°; melt shortening. Cook green pepper, onion, and meat, stirring occasionally, till vegetables are tender and meat is browned, about 5 minutes. Add bouillon, tomato sauce and seasonings to meat mixture; mix. Bring quickly to a boil; simmer uncovered 5 minutes. Add rice, mix well, cover. Reduce heat to about 220°. Cook till rice is tender, about 10 minutes. Makes 5 servings.

Beef-Eggplant Skillet

1 pound ground lean beef
¼ cup chopped onion
1 tablespoon all-purpose flour
1 8-ounce can (1 cup) seasoned
  tomato sauce
¾ cup water
¼ cup chopped green pepper
1 teaspoon oregano
½ to 1 teaspoon chili powder
½ teaspoon salt
. . .
1 small eggplant, cut in ½-inch slices
  (pared or unpared)
1 cup shredded sharp process cheese

Preheat electric skillet to about 375°. Brown beef and onion in small amount hot fat. Spoon off excess fat. Sprinkle flour over meat; stir. Add next 6 ingredients; mix well. Season eggplant with salt and pepper; arrange slices over meat. Cover; simmer at about 230° till eggplant is tender, 10 to 15 minutes. Top with shredded cheese. Pass grated Parmesan. Serves 4.

Savory Chicken Italiano

Tender chicken bubbles to just-right spicy goodness — in quick-from-a-mix spaghetti sauce! Bonus: Your electric skillet minds the main dish while you fix salad, dessert.

Chicken Italiano

Cut up one 2½- to 3-pound ready-to-cook frying chicken; salt lightly. Preheat electric skillet to about 360°. Add 2 tablespoons salad oil; add chicken; brown slowly, 15 to 20 minutes; spoon off fat.

Mix 1 envelope spaghetti-sauce mix according to directions, but *omitting extra fat;* pour over chicken. Cover; reduce heat to about 250°. Cook till tender, about 45 minutes, basting occasionally. Serves 4.

Lightning Lunch

1 12-ounce can luncheon meat
2 tablespoons butter or margarine
1 1-pound can whole yams, drained
4 canned cling peach halves
Dash cloves
¼ cup orange marmalade

Cut meat in 4 slices. Melt butter in electric skillet preheated to about 360°. Add meat, yams, and peaches; brown on one side. Turn; sprinkle yams with salt; and peaches with cloves. Spoon marmalade over meat. Heat uncovered at about 230°, basting often, till hot and glazed, about 5 minutes. Makes 4 servings.

Glazed Ham Dinner

Sunday dinner complete in a fry pan —

1 1-inch slice smoked ham
   (about 1½ pounds)
5 or 6 canned pineapple slices
2 medium acorn squash, cut in ¾-inch
   slices, halved
Salt

• • •

½ cup syrup from canned pinapple
½ cup pineapple preserves
2 teaspoons finely chopped
   candied ginger

Slash fat edge of ham at 2-inch intervals. Preheat electric skillet to about 360°. Brown ham slowly on one side, in small amount hot fat. Turn ham; overlap pineapple slices atop. Sprinkle squash with salt and arrange on either side of ham.

Combine ¼ *cup* pineapple syrup, the pineapple preserves, and candied ginger; drizzle over ham, pineapple, and squash.

Cover skillet; simmer at about 250° for 30 minutes or till squash is tender, spooning sauce over squash now and then, and adding remaining pineapple syrup if needed. Makes 5 to 6 servings.

Minute-steak Scramble

4 4-ounce cube steaks,
   cut in julienne strips
½ to 1 teaspoon ground ginger
¼ teaspoon salt
¼ teaspoon garlic salt
¼ cup salad oil
2 medium green peppers,
   cut in julienne strips
1 cup bias-cut celery slices
½ cup bias-cut green onion
. . .
2 tablespoons cornstarch
⅓ cup soy sauce
1 beef bouillon cube dissolved
   in 1 cup hot water
2 medium tomatoes, peeled and
   cut in eighths

Preheat electric skillet to about 350°. Season meat with ginger, salt, and garlic salt. Heat *half* the oil in skillet. Add meat; brown quickly on all sides. Remove meat. Add remaining oil; heat. Add peppers, celery, and green onion; cook just till slightly tender, about 5 minutes. Lower heat to about 250°. Combine cornstarch and soy sauce; stir in bouillon, and add to skillet. Cook and stir till mixture thickens and boils. Add meat and tomatoes; heat through, about 6 minutes. Serve with hot cooked rice. Makes 4 servings.

Shrimp Curry for a Crowd

½ cup butter or margarine
1½ cups chopped onion
1½ cups chopped celery
2 pounds cleaned, raw shrimp
   (about 3 pounds in shell),
   halved lengthwise
1 1-pound can (2 cups) applesauce
4 cans condensed cream of
   celery soup
1 6-ounce (1⅓ cups) can broiled
   sliced mushrooms, undrained
2 tablespoons curry powder
¼ teaspoon salt

Melt butter in 12-inch electric skillet preheated to about 300°. Add onion and celery; cook uncovered 5 minutes or till almost tender. Lower heat to simmering (220° to 240°); add remaining ingredients; stir. Simmer uncovered, stirring frequently, about 15 minutes. Makes 10 to 12 servings.

Sweet-Sour Tuna

Speedy sauce with an Oriental flair—

1 No. 2 can (2½ cups) pineapple
   chunks
¼ cup sugar
2 tablespoons cornstarch
½ teaspoon salt
1 chicken bouillon cube dissolved
   in 1 cup hot water
2 tablespoons vinegar
2 teaspoons soy sauce
. . .
1 green pepper, cut in
   ½-inch-wide strips
2 6½- or 7-ounce cans tuna, drained
   and broken in chunks
2 tablespoons butter or margarine
. . .
2 3-ounce cans chow-mein noodles

Preheat electric skillet to 230° to 250°. Drain pineapple, reserving syrup. Combine sugar, cornstarch, and salt; stir in bouillon, pineapple syrup, vinegar, soy sauce. Pour into skillet. Cook and stir till mixture bubbles. Continue cooking 1 minute.

Add pineapple, green pepper, tuna, and butter. Cover and simmer about 10 minutes, stirring occasionally. Serve over chow-mein noodles. Pass soy sauce. Serves 6.

Fresh-fruit Compote

Apples and pears take on pretty glaze; orange slices add refreshing flavor—

4 medium baking apples
4 ripe pears
2 unpeeled medium oranges, sliced
Seedless raisins
. . .
1 cup brown sugar
1 cup water
3 tablespoons butter or margarine

Core apples; pare a strip off top of each. If necessary, cut thin slice off bottom of pears so they'll stand upright. Arrange apples, pears, and orange slices in electric skillet; fill apple centers with raisins. Combine brown sugar and water; pour over fruits. Add butter. Bring to boiling; lower heat to simmering (about 220°) and cook covered 40 to 50 minutes or till done. Baste with the syrup now and then. Serves 8.

French-fried Onion Rings

Pour salad oil into electric skillet to depth of ¾ inch (about 4 cups). Heat oil to 375°. Peel 2 large onions, slice crosswise in ¼-inch slices. Separate in rings. Combine 1 unbeaten egg white, ½ cup milk, ½ cup sifted all-purpose flour, and dash salt; beat with a fork till smooth.

Dip rings one at a time into batter; drop in hot oil. Fry a few at a time for 2 or 3 minutes, or till golden brown, turning once. Drain on paper towels; season with salt. Keep warm in slow oven (200°) on rack, till ready to serve. Makes 4 servings.

Skillet Custards

Combine 3 slightly beaten eggs, ¼ cup sugar, and ¼ teaspoon salt; slowly stir in 2 cups slightly cooled scalded milk. Add ½ teaspoon vanilla. Pour into six 5-ounce buttered custard cups; dash with nutmeg.

Place cups on rack in preheated electric skillet. Cover and bake at 380°* about 25 to 30 minutes or till knife inserted off-center comes out clean. Top with tart jelly; serve warm in cups. Or chill and invert.

*Or heat as manufacturer suggests.

Dessert Dumplings

Your electric saucepan is the helper here—

¾ cup sugar

. . .

2½ cups hot water
¾ cup sugar
¼ teaspoon salt
1 teaspoon vanilla

. . .

1 cup packaged biscuit mix
2 tablespoons sugar
⅓ cup milk
⅓ cup chopped California walnuts

Preheat electric saucepan to about 400°. Add ¾ cup sugar; melt, stirring constantly until amber-colored. Turn off heat; stir until liquid thickens and cools slightly. Slowly stir in water; add ¾ cup sugar, the salt, and vanilla; mix well.

With fork, combine biscuit mix, 2 tablespoons sugar, milk, and nuts, stirring until just moistened. Heat syrup to simmering; then drop batter in by rounded teaspoons, making 8 dumplings. Cover and cook at low heat (about 150°) 6 to 8 minutes, or till dumplings are done. Let cool slightly before serving. Serves 8.

Skillet Biscuits—for a quick breakfast or a late evening snack—

Skillet Biscuits: These look almost like tiny English muffins.

Preheat electric skillet to 380° and grease lightly with butter or margarine.

Place biscuits in skillet—don't let them touch each other. Cover and bake 3 minutes. Turn biscuits; cover and bake about 3 minutes longer. Serve hot with butter and your favorite jelly, jam, or preserves.

Buzz it in the blender

Gourmet Chicken Soup

1 can condensed cream of
  chicken soup
1 *cup* canned condensed chicken
  consomme
½ teaspoon tarragon
½ cup heavy cream

Blend ingredients till smooth, about 10
seconds. Heat through. Serve hot. *Or*, chill;
serve topped with whipped cream sprin-
kled with paprika. Makes 4 or 5 servings.

Blender Borsch

*Serve this shocking-pink soup ice-cold from
blender—*

1 cup dairy sour cream
1 1-pound can (2 cups) diced beets,
  chilled and drained
1 ½-inch slice lemon, peeled
½ small onion, sliced
½ teaspoon salt
½ teaspoon sugar
1 cup crushed ice

To blender, add ¾ *cup* of the sour cream,
the beets, lemon, onion, salt, and sugar.
Cover and blend at high speed about 15
seconds. Scrape down sides of container
and add the ice.

  Cover and blend about 10 seconds longer.
Serve immediately, topped with dollops of
remaining sour cream. Makes 5 servings.

Speedy Pea Soup

1 1-pound can (2 cups) green peas
1 cup light cream (or ¾ cup milk
  and ¼ cup light cream)
¼ medium onion
2 tablespoons butter or margarine
¼ teaspoon salt
Dash pepper

Heat green peas (with liquid) and cream.
Empty into blender. Add onion, butter or
margarine, salt, and pepper. Blend till
smooth, about 1 minute. Pour from container right into soup bowls. Top with
croutons. Makes 3 or 4 servings.

Red-raspberry Fluff

1 3-ounce package red-raspberry
  gelatin
½ cup boiling water
1 cup *drained* crushed ice

Empty gelatin into blender. Add boiling
water; cover. Blend 2 minutes to dissolve.
Keep blender running; slowly add ice. Then
blend 1 minute or till container feels cool.
Pour into *chilled* sherbets.* Wait 5 minutes,
then serve pronto! Serves 4 to 6.

  *To match picture: Dip rims of glasses
in raspberry juice (from frozen, or a few
crushed fresh, berries), then in sugar, before chilling. Pour Fluff over thawed frozen
or fresh berries; trim with berries and mint.

Pimiento Salad Dressing

1 4-ounce can pimientos, *un*drained
⅓ cup salad oil
¼ cup vinegar
2 tablespoons crumbled blue cheese
1½ teaspoons sugar
½ teaspoon salt
1 thin slice onion
4 whole black peppers

Blend all ingredients about 10 seconds or
until smooth at low or medium speed.
Chill; serve on lettuce, cucumber slices, or
grapefruit sections. Makes about 1¼ cups.

3-Cheese Dip

¼ cup water
1 cup cream-style cottage cheese
2 3-ounce packages cream cheese,
  softened
2 tablespoons crumbled blue cheese
1 small clove garlic
Few drops bottled hot pepper sauce

Pour water into blender. Add cottage
cheese; cover and blend at high speed
about 20 seconds. Stop motor.

  Add remaining ingredients. Cover;
blend 30 seconds or till smooth. Pass with
crackers. Makes about 2 cups.

Red-raspberry Fluff   This delightful dessert is simply gelatin, water, and crushed ice, all blended to a light airy foam. For a party, serve over berries; rim glasses with raspberry-flavored sugar crystals.

Crunchy Pecan Waffles

Serve for dessert or special occasion—

2 eggs
1½ cups milk
¼ cup salad oil
2 cups sifted all-purpose flour
3 teaspoons baking powder
1 teaspoon sugar
¼ teaspoon salt
Pecan halves

Place eggs, milk, and salad oil in blender. Cover and run at high speed until creamy (about 30 seconds). Add remaining ingredients except pecans and mix at high speed until smooth (1½ minutes).

Preheat electric waffle baker. Pour mixture onto hot waffle grid. Sprinkle with pecan halves. Bake till golden brown. Makes about 6 medium waffles or 12 small squares.

Orange or Lemon Sugar

Place 2½ tablespoons coarsely snipped orange or lemon peel (white part removed) in blender; add ½ cup sugar. Blend 5 seconds or till peel is in tiny flecks. With a spoon, stir in 1 cup additional sugar. Serve with tea, or sprinkle on sugar cookies.

Pink Parfait Pie

See this high-piled beauty on page 4—

1 3-ounce package strawberry-
    flavored gelatin
¾ cup boiling water
1 10-ounce package frozen
    sliced strawberries
1 pint strawberry ice cream
1 8-inch whole-vanilla-wafer crust

Empty gelatin into blender, add boiling water, let stand 10 seconds to soften. Cover, blend 10 seconds or till dissolved.

Cut package of frozen strawberries in half. Set aside half for topping; allow to thaw. Add other half to gelatin mixture along with ice cream; blend till smooth, about 20 seconds. Chill 5 to 10 minutes, or till mixture mounds when spooned, stirring occasionally. Pile into cooky crust; chill 3 to 4 hours or till firm. Garnish with whipped cream and strawberries to match picture. Makes 6 servings.

Cheesecake

Crust:
4 zwieback crackers
1 tablespoon sugar
1 tablespoon soft butter or
    margarine

Break *half* the zwieback into blender container. Add sugar and butter. Blend, stopping and starting motor several times if needed. Break in remaining zwieback and blend. Butter sides of a 6-inch spring-form pan*, press crumb mixture on bottom.

Filling:
1 envelope (1 tablespoon)
    unflavored gelatin
1 thin strip lemon peel
2 tablespoons lemon juice
½ teaspoon vanilla
Dash salt
½ cup *hot* milk

• • •

½ cup sugar
2 egg yolks
1 8-ounce package cream cheese,
    cut in fourths
1 cup drained crushed ice
½ cup whipping cream

In blender, put gelatin, lemon peel, and juice, vanilla, salt, and hot milk. Cover and blend at high speed about 40 seconds. Add sugar, egg yolks, and cream cheese. Cover and blend at high speed 10 seconds. Add ice and cream; cover and blend about 15 seconds more or till smooth. Carefully pour into crumb-lined pan. Chill at least 3 hours. Remove sides of pan and garnish cheesecake with whipped cream and canned mandarin oranges. Serves 6.

*Or pour filling into 10x6x1½-inch baking dish, sprinkle crumb mixture over top. To serve, cut in squares.

Quick Banana Drink

2 medium ripe bananas
2 cups milk
2 large scoops vanilla ice cream

Break banana into blender container. Blend till smooth, about 15 seconds; scrape down sides. Add milk and ice cream. Buzz till blended, about 15 seconds. Serves 3 or 4.

Ice-cooked Chocolate Bavarian

1½ envelopes (1½ tablespoons)
   unflavored gelatin
2 teaspoons instant coffee powder
¼ cup cold water
½ cup hot water

   • • •

1 6-ounce package (1 cup)
   semisweet chocolate pieces
1 tablespoon sugar
Dash salt
½ teaspoon vanilla
2 egg yolks
1¼ cups *drained* finely crushed ice
1 cup whipping cream

In blender, put gelatin, instant coffee, cold water, and hot water. Cover and blend at high speed about 40 seconds. Add chocolate, sugar, salt, and vanilla; cover and blend about 10 seconds more or till smooth.

Keeping motor running, remove cover; add egg yolks, crushed ice, and cream; blend 20 more seconds or till dessert begins to thicken. Pour into sherbets; chill about 10 minutes; serve. Makes 6 servings.

Jiffy Milk-chocolate Frosting

1 cup sugar
3 1-ounce squares unsweetened
   chocolate, cut in small pieces
1 6-ounce can evaporated milk

Put sugar in blender; cover and blend about 1 minute at high speed. Add chocolate, evaporated milk, and dash salt; blend at high speed about 3 minutes or till thick, using rubber spatula to scrape sides as necessary. Frosts tops of two 8-inch layers. (For firmer frosting, chill frosted cake.)

Easy Chocolate Frosting

1 6-ounce package (1 cup)
   semisweet chocolate pieces
½ cup soft butter or margarine
¼ cup hot water
4 egg yolks
2 tablespoons confectioners' sugar
1 teaspoon vanilla

In blender, combine all ingredients. Blend at high speed till smooth. Frosts tops of two 8-inch layers. (If firmer frosting is desired, chill frosted cake.)

Mocha Shake

A rich, creamy, coffee-flavored drink. Remember it for hot summer days—

1 pint chocolate ice cream
2 cups milk
2 tablespoons instant coffee powder
¼ teaspoon nutmeg
Whipped cream
Instant coffee or nutmeg

Place first 4 ingredients in blender. Cover and blend until smooth, about 1 minute. Pour immediately into mugs. Top with fluffs of whipped cream; sprinkle with instant coffee or nutmeg. Makes 4 cups.

One-step Sherbet

Use one 10-ounce package frozen raspberries *or* one 13½-ounce can frozen pineapple chunks. Break up frozen fruit, place in blender. Turn blender on. With rubber spatula, work fruit down slowly until smooth and of sherbet consistency (about 1 minute for raspberries, 3 minutes for pineapple). Serve immediately.

For more solid sherbet, empty into refrigerator tray, freeze till ready to serve. Makes about 3 servings.

Blender tips

Meat Sandwich Spread: Cut leftover ham or roast beef in small pieces, add mayonnaise, and 2 or 3 sweet pickles. Cover; blend. Celery stalk is dandy "spatula" for pushing mixture into blades.

Buttered Crumbs: Cut dry or soft bread in small pieces. Place in blender. Add soft butter or margarine (½ tablespoon per slice of bread). Blend.

To smooth lumpy gravy or white sauce: Just pour hot mixture into blender and let motor run about ½ to 1 minute.

Grated cheese: Add cubes or pieces of cheese (just out of the refrigerator) through insert opening while blades are in motion. (Drop small amount at a time.) Blend few seconds. *Note:* Cheese must be cold or it will pack at bottom of container.

Electric deep-fat fryer

Fried Peach Pies

1 1-pound can sliced peaches,
    well drained (1½ cups)
3 tablespoons honey
2 tablespoons butter or margarine
1 teaspoon shredded lemon peel
1 tablespoon lemon juice
¼ teaspoon cinnamon
1 package refrigerated biscuits

Combine first 6 ingredients. Cook over medium heat, stirring frequently, till thick and glossy (about 15 minutes). Separate biscuits; roll each to an oval shape, about 5 inches long. Place a rounded tablespoon of filling just off center, lengthwise, of each biscuit. Fold dough over and thoroughly seal edges with tines of fork.

Fry in deep hot fat (375°), turning once about 1 minute. Drain; sprinkle with confectioners' sugar. Makes 10.

Electric mixer

No-Bake Lemon Pie

1½ cups fine graham-cracker crumbs
¼ cup sugar
½ cup melted butter
1 15-ounce can (1⅓ cups)
    sweetened condensed milk
1 egg
1 teaspoon grated lemon peel
½ cup lemon juice
Trim (optional)

Make crust: Combine crumbs, sugar, and melted butter. Press into buttered 8-inch pie plate. Chill till firm, about 45 minutes.

In mixing bowl, combine condensed milk, egg, lemon peel, and lemon juice. Beat a few seconds till mixture thickens. Spread filling in chilled crust. Chill till firm. Add trim, if desired.

Trim: Center pie with a fluffy mound of green-tinted whipped cream, circled with a few kumquat "tulips" and sprigs of green leaves. To fashion a pair of "tulips," cut a preserved kumquat in half lengthwise; slit one end of each half in three places to form petals. Place cut-side down on pie.

Electric salad maker

Country Coleslaw

Using salad maker, shred cabbage and carrots to make 3 cups shredded cabbage and 1 cup shredded carrots. Crisp on ice for an hour. Drain. Toss with ⅔ cup Coleslaw Dressing. Makes 6 servings.

Coleslaw Dressing

1 6-ounce can evaporated milk
⅓ cup sugar
⅓ cup vinegar
1 egg
1 teaspoon celery seed
1 teaspoon salt
Dash pepper

Blend ingredients till smooth, about 10 seconds. Pour into saucepan; cook and stir till thick. Chill. Makes 1⅓ cups.

Electric saucepan

Hungarian Goulash

⅓ cup fat
1½ pounds lean beef chuck, cut
    in 1-inch cubes
1 cup chopped onion
1 tablespoon all-purpose flour
¾ teaspoon salt
1 tablespoon paprika
1 can condensed beef broth plus
    water to make 2 cups
1 8-ounce can seasoned tomato sauce
1 1-pound can (2 cups) tomatoes
1 clove garlic, minced
Bouquet Garni*

Preheat electric saucepan to about 400°; melt fat; brown beef and cook onions till just tender. Add flour, salt and paprika; cook and stir 5 minutes. Add remaining ingredients; heat to boiling.

Cover; turn heat to 150° to 200° and simmer till meat is tender, about 1¼ hours, stirring occasionally. Remove Bouquet Garni; serve with hot macaroni. Serves 6.

Bouquet Garni: 1 bay leaf, 1 stalk celery, few sprigs parsley, and 1 blade or dash thyme, all tied in a cheesecloth bag.

Electric ice-cream freezer

Pineapple Ice Cream

    1 cup dairy sour cream
    1 15-ounce can (1⅓ cups)
        sweetened condensed milk
    2 cups milk
    1 9-ounce can crushed pineapple

Combine sour cream and sweetened condensed milk; add milk. Freeze in 2-quart electric ice-cream freezer, using 6 parts ice to 1 part salt, till partially frozen. Add pineapple (with syrup); freeze.

    Remove the dasher. Cover the freezer can with several thicknesses of waxed paper; replace lid. Pack in ice and salt; allow to ripen 1 hour. (Or ripen ice cream in refrigerator tray.) Makes 2 quarts.

Vanilla Custard Ice Cream

    ¾ cup sugar
    3 tablespoons all-purpose flour
    2 cups milk
    2 beaten eggs
    2 cups whipping cream
    1½ tablespoons vanilla

Combine sugar, flour, and dash salt; gradually stir in milk. Cook, stirring constantly, till thick. Add small amount of hot mixture to eggs and mix well; return to hot mixture; cook and stir 1 minute. Chill. Add remaining ingredients.

    Freeze in 2-quart (or larger) electric ice cream freezer, using 6 parts ice to 1 part salt. Remove dasher.

    Cover freezer can with several thicknesses of waxed paper; replace lid. Pack in ice and salt; let ripen a few hours. (Or ripen in freezing unit.) Makes 1¼ quarts.

Electric rotisserie

Rotisserie Appetizers

    Cut a loaf of canned luncheon meat in 4 squares; string on spit. Let turn on rotisserie till hot through, brushing often with Glaze. Remove meat and cut in bite-size cubes. Insert toothpicks; serve.

    Glaze: Melt 2 tablespoons butter; add ¼ cup syrup from canned fruit and ¼ cup brown sugar; bring to boiling. It's ready!

Electric waffle baker

Wonderful Waffles

    2¼ cups sifted all-purpose flour
    4 teaspoons baking powder
    ¾ teaspoon salt
    1½ tablespoons sugar
    2 beaten eggs
    2¼ cups milk
    ¾ cup salad oil or melted shortening

Sift together dry ingredients. Combine eggs, milk, and salad oil; add to dry ingredients just before baking. Beat only until dry ingredients are moistened. (This is a thin batter.) Bake in preheated waffle baker. Makes 10 to 12 waffles.

    Note: If you like a heartier waffle, use 2½ cups sifted all-purpose flour.

Keep them humming

Safety first!

When using electrical small appliances:
• Plug cord into *appliance* first, then into wall, to prevent sparks. Disconnect cord from wall before unplugging appliance.
• Keep appliance cords dry.
• Make sure appliance cords don't dangle where children can reach them.
• Don't yank appliance cords from outlets. Be sure to grasp the plug firmly with fingers.
• Too many appliances plugged into the same circuit can blow a fuse quickly.
• Use handy tongs to turn frying food or to remove food from hot water.
• Watch deep fat so it doesn't overheat.

More electric maids at your service

Bean pot	Ice crusher
Bun warmer	Instant coffee
Can opener	and tea maker
Coffee maker	Juicer
Corn popper	Knife sharpener
Drink mixer	Hot tray
Dutch oven	Roaster
Egg cooker	Portable broiler
Food grinder	Portable oven
Grill	Pressure pan
Hot-dog cooker	Toaster

Bests from the broiler

On days when you've a jillion things to do, draft your broiler to help you get a fast, but fabulous, meal. Tender meat, vegetables, and fruit accompaniments cook all at once. Later, you can even broil dessert!

A hearty broiler meal, ready in 25 minutes

← Everything's sizzling hot — Mixed Grill with Vegetables offers three meats, potatoes, cheese-topped tomatoes. Rest of dinner's a snap — toss a crisp salad, tuck foil-wrapped rolls in the oven to heat. Fix Strawberry Pudding Cakes while meal broils.

Bigtime broiler meals

Your broiler does the work—dinner's on the table in no time at all

> ### Lamb-chop Broil
>
> Mixed Grill with Vegetables
> Tossed Green Salad
> French Dressing
> Hot Rolls   Butter
> Strawberry Pudding Cakes Coffee

Strawberry Pudding Cakes

Stir up a package of instant vanilla pudding and allow to set; add 1 cup drained, sugared, sliced strawberries.

Spoon most of pudding into four sponge-cake dessert cups. Top each with a chilled canned peach half, a dab of the remaining pudding, and a big berry with green cap. Makes 4 quick, colorful servings.

1 *Mixed Grill with Vegetables:* Score fat edge of five 1-inch *lamb chops*. String tiny canned or cooked *potatoes* on skewers; brush with butter. Broil 4 inches from heat 10 minutes. Meanwhile, simmer 8 *sausage links* in ¼ cup water in covered skillet 5 minutes; drain. Season chops and potatoes; turn. Add sausage to rack; broil about 5 minutes.

2 While chops, sausage, and potatoes broil, halve 2 *tomatoes*; score cut surface, making ½-inch squares. Mix ½ cup soft bread crumbs and ¼ cup shredded process cheese; sprinkle on tomatoes. Arrange tomatoes and 8 slices bacon on broiler rack. Turn sausage. Butter potatoes again—dash with paprika. Return to broiler till bacon is done.

3 *Tossed Green Salad:* Get washed, chilled greens from refrigerator. Tear leaf and head lettuce and endive into salad bowl.

Add slices of radish, green onion, and unpared cucumber for fresh-from-the-garden flavor and crunch. Toss salad lightly with your favorite French dressing (bottled or from a mix) at the table, so it stays crisp.

Circle Pups

It's the cut that makes 'em curl—

1 1-pound can (2 cups) sauerkraut
1 tablespoon flour
1 teaspoon sage
• • •
1 pound (8-10) frankfurters*
8 to 10 slices rye bread, buttered
Prepared mustard

Drain sauerkraut, reserving ½ cup juice. Mix flour, sage, and reserved juice; stir into the drained kraut. Heat and stir till the mixture thickens.

At ½-inch intervals, cut slits across franks, *going almost but not quite through.* Broil franks until hot through—they'll curl as they cook!

Place franks on bread; fill center with hot sauerkraut; top with mustard. Makes 4 or 5 servings (2 apiece).

*If using the chubby dinner-size franks, count on 2 to make each circle. Curve on bread with ends touching; fill.

Peach Melba Dessert

Chill canned peach halves; drain. For each serving place a peach half in a sherbet dish. Top with a scoop of vanilla or peach ice cream. Spoon prepared black raspberry topping (from jar) over all.

Hot-'n-Cold Dessert Waffles

Double topping—crunchy broiled coconut plus a big scoop of ice cream—

¼ cup butter or margarine
½ cup brown sugar
½ cup flaked or shredded coconut
• • •
6 frozen baked waffles
Ice cream (vanilla, maple nut, or butter crunch)

Combine butter, brown sugar, and coconut. Spread on frozen waffles, and broil 4 inches from heat till bubbly and golden, about 7 minutes. Top with ice cream and serve immediately! Makes 6 servings.

Teen Topper: Spread each frozen waffle with 1 tablespoon peanut butter; top with 2 marshmallows, halved. Broil till golden.

Family Favorite

Treasure-burgers *or* Circle Pups
Miniature Potatoes and
Special Green Beans
Celery and Carrot Sticks
Peach Melba Dessert *or*
Hot-'n-Cold Dessert Waffles
Coffee   Cocoa

Treasure-burgers

1 pound ground beef
Pepper process-cheese food
¼ cup chopped ripe olives
4 strips bacon

Shape meat in eight 4-inch patties. Leaving a ½-inch margin, center *half* of patties with two thin slices of cheese food and 1 tablespoon olives each. Cover with remaining patties; press edges to seal. Toothpick bacon around edge of each.

Arrange burgers on broiler-pan rack. Broil 4 inches from heat 8 minutes. Sprinkle with salt and pepper. Turn; broil 5 minutes longer, or until done. Season with salt and pepper to taste.

Miniature Potatoes and Special Green Beans

Vegetables broil on rack alongside burgers. Sour-cream topping makes beans "special"—

Put contents of 1-pound package frozen miniature potato patties, one layer deep, at one end of a shallow pan—you can make it of foil. Drizzle with 2 tablespoons melted butter or margarine.

Drain one 1-pound can green beans, place at other end of pan (separate from potatoes with foil; or use two pans). Drizzle with 1 tablespoon melted butter.

Place pan of vegetables on broiler-pan rack. Broil 4 inches from heat 8 minutes. Sprinkle beans with salt and pepper. Turn potatoes, stir beans; broil 5 minutes longer, or till done. Spoon ½ cup dairy sour cream over beans just before serving.

Ham Slice—Broiler Fast

Glazed Ham with Potato Patties
or Ham with Potatoes and Pineapple
Buttered Mexican-style Corn
Cool Cucumber Molds
Hard Rolls   Butter
Vanilla Ice Cream   Sugar Cookies
Hot Coffee

Hint: Make salad the night before.
Ham and potatoes go in the broiler
while the corn heats atop the range.

Glazed Ham with Potato Patties

½ cup apricot jam or preserves
¼ teaspoon salt
1 tablespoon water
1 ¾-inch slice *fully cooked* ham
  (about 1 pound)
1 12-ounce package frozen
  potato patties
3 tablespoons butter, melted
Salt and paprika

Mix first 3 ingredients. Slash fat edge of
ham slice. Place ham and potato patties on
broiler-pan rack. Spread *half* the apricot
glaze on ham; brush potatoes with *half* the
butter. Broil 3 inches from heat 6 minutes.
Turn ham and patties. Spread ham with
remaining glaze. Butter patties; season.
Broil 6 minutes more. Serves 4.

Ham with Potatoes and Pineapple

Select a ¾-inch *fully cooked* ham slice.
Score edge of ham slice about ¼ inch deep
in several places.
 Place ham slice, canned sweet-potato
halves, and pineapple rings on broiler
rack. Brush potatoes and pineapple with
melted butter. Place 3 inches from heat.
 Broil 6 minutes; turn ham. Place a
canned spiced crab apple in center of each
pineapple ring. Brush potatoes and pineapple with melted butter. Broil 6 minutes
more. Serve on warmed platter.

Cool Cucumber Molds

1 3-ounce package lemon-flavored
  gelatin
1 cup boiling water
1 cup cold water
2 tablespoons lemon juice
¼ teaspoon salt
1 large unpared cucumber
¼ cup chopped green onions

Dissolve gelatin in boiling water. Add cold
water, lemon juice, and salt. Chill till partially set. Meanwhile, halve cucumber and
scrape out seeds; shred cucumber (you'll
need 1½ cups *drained* shredded cucumber).
Stir in shredded cucumber and onions.
Pour into 5 individual molds. Chill till
firm. Makes 5 servings.

Broiled Lamb Dinner

Broiled Lamb Chops Parmesan
Minted Pears
Tossed Green Salad
Brown-and-serve Rolls   Butter
Lemon Sherbet   Coffee

Broiled Lamb Chops Parmesan

6 lamb chops, about ¾ inch thick
¼ cup grated Parmesan cheese
2 tablespoons soft butter or margarine
½ teaspoon salt
Dash pepper

Broil chops 3 to 4 inches from heat 8 to 10
minutes or till lightly browned. Turn; broil
4 to 5 minutes or to desired doneness.
Blend remaining ingredients; spread on
chops. Broil 1 to 2 minutes or till cheese is
lightly browned. Makes 6 servings.

Minted Pears

 Place canned pear halves, hollow side
up, beside lamb chops when you turn
chops. Fill with mint jelly same time you
spread chops with cheese mixture. Broil
1 to 2 minutes more. Serve with chops.

Grand broiler main dish, crisp relishes and speedy dessert make quick meal.

Dessert is steamed pudding. Simply slip a can of steamed pudding into boiling water —let simmer according to label directions. Come dessert time, team hot pudding with *Frosty Sauce:* Beat 1 pint soft vanilla ice cream till fluffy. Dash with nutmeg.

Cranburger Broil

Cranburgers
Green Beans
Buttered Sweet Potato Halves
Stuffed Olives
Carrot Sticks   Celery Sticks
Steamed Fig Pudding
with Frosty Sauce
Hot Coffee

Cranburger Broil

Green Beans: Drain canned green beans, put in broiler *pan.* Warm 5 inches from heat while you fix burgers.

Cranburgers: Pour one 6-ounce can evaporated milk over 2 slices white bread; add 1½ pounds ground beef, 2 tablespoons instant minced onion, 1½ teaspoons salt, ¼ teaspoon pepper. Mix; form 6 patties.

To complete: Place patties on broiler *rack;* broil 6 minutes. Turn patties and add canned *sweet-potato halves.* Brush potatoes with melted butter; season. Broil 5 minutes. Top each patty with 1 tablespoon whole cranberry sauce. Broil 2 minutes.

Patties broil above; green beans heat below.

Sweet potatoes get basting of melted butter.

Aloha Broiled Chicken— This broiler meals looks like a million *and* tastes like it— for little effort. Here the golden chicken and grilled fruits get last-minute trim—snipped parsley, crab apples.

Broiled Peanut Topper

Blend ¼ cup peanut butter, ¼ cup light cream, and 1 cup brown sugar; spread over warm 8- or 9-inch square cake. Sprinkle with ½ cup flaked coconut. Broil 4 to 5 inches from heat about 4 minutes or till frosting is lightly browned. Serve warm.

Aloha Broiled Chicken

Select two 2-pound ready-to-cook broiler chickens; split in half. Brush with melted butter; season. Place skin side down on broiler pan (no rack). Broil 5 to 7 inches from heat, 25 minutes, or till lightly browned. Brush occasionally with melted butter. Turn; broil 15 to 20 minutes longer.

About 5 minutes before end of cooking time, place canned pineapple rings and peach halves beside chicken. Brush chicken and fruits with Pineapple Sauce; broil 5 minutes. Pass with the sauce. Serves 4.

Pineapple Sauce: Melt ½ cup butter, blend in 1 teaspoon cornstarch. Add 1 teaspoon grated lemon peel, ¼ cup lemon juice, ⅓ cup pineapple syrup, 2 tablespoons finely chopped onion, 1 teaspoon soy sauce, and ¼ teaspoon thyme. Cook 5 minutes over low heat, stirring constantly.

Broiler recipe roundup

Herb Chicken

2 1½- to 2½-pound ready-to-cook
  chickens, split in half
⅔ cup salad oil
2 tablespoons chopped parsley
1 teaspoon salt
1 teaspoon seasoned salt
½ teaspoon marjoram
½ teaspoon paprika
¼ teaspoon *each* pepper and tarragon

Place chicken in shallow pan. Mix remaining ingredients; pour over chicken and let stand 2 hours, turning occasionally. Drain off marinade and reserve.

Place chicken skin side down on broiler pan (no rack). Broil 7 inches from heat about 25 minutes, basting occasionally. Turn; broil 15 to 20 minutes longer. Chicken's done when thick part of drumstick cuts easily with no pink showing. Serves 4.

Broiler Banquet

2 ready-to-cook broiler chickens
  (2 pounds each), split in half
¼ cup butter, melted
1 teaspoon salt
¼ teaspoon monosodium glutamate
   • • •
½ cup currant jelly
¼ cup frozen orange-juice concentrate
1½ teaspoons cornstarch
1 teaspoon dry mustard
Dash bottled hot pepper sauce

Brush chicken with melted butter; season with salt and monosodium glutamate.

Place skin side down in broiler pan (without rack). Broil 7 inches from heat 25 minutes or till lightly browned. Turn; broil 15 to 20 minutes or till tender, brushing last few minutes with Currant-Orange Sauce. Serve with Fluffy Orange Rice.

Currant-Orange Sauce: Combine jelly, concentrate and ¼ cup water; heat and stir till smooth. Blend together cornstarch, dry mustard, hot pepper sauce, and 1 tablespoon cold water; stir into jelly mixture. Cook and stir till the sauce thickens.

Fluffy Orange Rice

1 cup chopped celery
¼ cup chopped onion
¼ cup butter
   • • •
2 tablespoons orange-juice
  concentrate
1¼ cups water
½ teaspoons salt
1⅓ cups packaged precooked rice

Cook celery and onion in butter till tender. Add concentrate, water, and salt.

Bring to boiling; add rice; continue as directed on package. Makes 4 servings.

Garlic-broiled Tomatoes

4 medium tomatoes
1 to 2 tablespoons butter, melted
Garlic salt

Turn tomatoes stem end down and cut crisscross mark, about ⅓ through.

Brush with melted butter and sprinkle with garlic salt. Broil 4 inches from heat 10 to 15 minutes. Makes 4 servings.

Broiled Coconut Frosting

⅔ cup brown sugar
⅓ cup melted butter or margarine
¼ cup light cream
1 3½-ounce can (1⅓ cups)
  flaked coconut
½ teaspoon vanilla

Thoroughly combine all ingredients. Spread over warm 9-inch square cake. Brown lightly in broiler. Serve while warm.

Broiled Cream Topper

1 cup dairy sour cream
½ cup brown sugar
¼ cup chopped walnuts

Mix sour cream and sugar. Spread over a warm 9-inch square cake in pan.

Sprinkle with nuts. Broil 3 inches from heat about 2 minutes or till frosting is set.

Sausage 'n Peach Special

Drain 1 No. 2½ can (3½ cups) peach halves. Sprinkle each peach half with brown sugar. Broil 3 inches from heat 5 minutes. Put chili sauce in each peach half; top with 2 Vienna sausages. Broil 8 to 10 minutes more. Makes 6 to 8 servings.

Surprise Logs

Inside each, a row of olives. Next time, the surprise can be a dill pickle stick—

1 pound ground beef
¼ cup packaged corn-flake crumbs, or finely crushed corn flakes
¼ cup dairy sour cream
2 tablespoons chili sauce
2 tablespoons chopped ripe olives
2 tablespoons chopped onion
1 tablespoon snipped parsley
½ teaspoon salt
Dash pepper
. . .
20 pitted ripe olives
. . .
5 coney buns, toasted

Combine first 9 ingredients; shape in 5 logs to fit coney buns. Press a row of olives into center of each log, molding meat around olives.

Broil 3 inches from heat, turning occasionally, 12 to 15 minutes or till done. Serve in coney buns. Makes 5 servings.

Broiled Rock-lobster Tails

Partially thaw frozen lobster tails. To butterfly, snip through center of hard top shell with kitchen scissors. With sharp knife cut through meat but *not through under shell*. Spread open.

Place on broiler rack, shell down. (Protect tail "fans" by covering with foil.) Brush meat with melted butter—dash in few drops bottled hot pepper sauce. Broil 4 to 5 inches from heat 10 to 20 minutes for tails under 8 ounces; 15 to 25 minutes for larger ones. Brush often with butter while cooking. Lobster is done when you can flake it with fork.

Insert fork between shell and meat, lift to give built-up look. Brush with butter.

Garlic Lamb Kabobs

1½ pounds boneless lamb shoulder, cut in 1-inch cubes
. . .
1 cup garlic salad dressing or 1 envelope garlic dressing mix*
. . .
2 medium green peppers, cut in wedges
1 1-pound can (2 cups) small whole onions

Place meat in shallow dish; pour dressing over. Let stand, turning occasionally, 2 hours at room temperature.

Run eight 12-inch skewers through meat fat to grease. Thread on skewers in this order: lamb, green pepper, lamb, onion. Broil 4 inches from heat, 10 to 15 minutes, turning once and brushing occasionally with marinade. Makes 8 servings.

Go-withs: Fluffy rice, crisp relishes, and toasted French bread slices.

*Prepare mix using label directions.

Southern Steak Bar-B-Q

Butter-brown steak in skillet first, then glaze to a fine finish in broiler—

¼ cup soft butter or margarine
2 tablespoons dry mustard
2 teaspoons salt
2 teaspoons sugar
¾ teaspoon paprika
¼ teaspoon pepper
. . .
2 pounds 1-inch sirloin steak
. . .
¼ cup olive oil
2 tablespoons Worcestershire sauce
2 tablespoons catsup
¾ teaspoon sugar
¾ teaspoon salt

For seasoned butter, mix first 6 ingredients; spread *half* on one side of steak. In large skillet, brown meat buttered side down. As this browns, spread remaining butter over top; turn and brown.

Remove to broiler. For sauce, mix remaining ingredients; add skillet drippings; brush on steak. Broil 5 inches from heat 5 to 7 minutes on each side, brushing frequently with sauce. Makes 6 servings.

Classic—Planked Steak

This thick steak with fluffy potato border is special-occasion. At Chicago's Stock Yard Inn, it comes complete with peas and carrots, French-fried onions, grilled tomato!

Planked Steak

Choose a porterhouse, T-bone, or sirloin steak, 1½ inches thick. Slash fatty edge at intervals—don't cut into meat.

Place steak on broiler rack; broil top side, season with salt and pepper. Turn, broil other side. Remove from oven about 7 minutes before steak is done the way you like it (allow 15-20 minutes *total* for rare; 20-30 minutes for medium). Place steak on seasoned plank. Pipe border of Duchess Potatoes around meat, using pastry tube. Broil potatoes with meat about 7 minutes. (*Or*, bake at 450° about 12 minutes.)

Remove from broiler (or oven); add hot buttered vegetables (your choice) and parsley. Top steak with a pat or two of butter. Place plank on serving tray. Serves 4.

To season plank (you can do this while steak broils): Place oak plank in shallow pan; cover with hot water. Let stand a few minutes. Remove; dry with a towel. Brush plank well with salad oil.

Duchess Potatoes

To 4 cups hot mashed potatoes, add 1 tablespoon butter, 2 beaten egg yolks, and salt and white pepper to taste; mix well. Using pastry bag with No. 7 or 9 star tip, pipe hot potato mixture around *broiled* steak on plank. (To match picture, form loops to hold vegetables, too.)

Drizzle potatoes with 2 tablespoons butter, melted. Broil (meat and all) 4 inches from heat about 7 minutes (or bake at 450° for 12 minutes). Makes 6 to 8 servings.

5-minute Broiled Shrimp

Mince 3 large cloves garlic; cook in ¼ cup butter 2 or 3 minutes. Place 12 ounces raw cleaned shrimp, one layer deep, in foil-lined broiler pan. Dash with salt and pepper. Place ½ lemon, thinly sliced, over shrimp; drizzle with garlic butter.

Broil in preheated broiler 3 inches from heat 4 to 6 minutes or till done, brushing once with drippings. Serves 3 or 4.

Freeze ahead for free-time meals

Anticipate those no-time-to-cook days. Here are main dishes and fun desserts you stow in the freezer ahead, exciting fix-ups for the speedy ingredients offered by your grocer's frozen-foods case. You'll be ready to "heat and eat" anytime

Lunch, dinner, snack—easy from freezer

← Sesame-seeded Corned Beef Bunwiches are hearty midday fare, perfect teen-time snack, too. High-hat Meat Loaves are complete individual main dishes; relishes and sundaes complete the meal. For after bridge: Frozen Rainbow Dessert.

It's easy to freeze it

Your freezer's versatile—use it often. Double a recipe and freeze half, store leftovers, make frozen desserts. Tuck away seasonal or frozen-food bargains. You can short-order-chef-it anytime!

Are you "in-the-know" about making best use of your freezer? Scan these tips:

- Cool to-be-frozen foods like meat sauces and stews at once; set pan of cooked food in bowl or sink containing cold water with ice till room temperature; package.
- Wrap and freeze most foods, but freeze and *then* wrap ice cream, meringues, and whipped-cream desserts.
- Pack in family-size units, for ease of use *and* speedy freezing.
- Use moisture-vaporproof wrapping materials and containers. Seal *airtight*.
- Label each package clearly with contents, weight, and date of freezing.
- Don't crowd meat packages in the freezer. It slows down freezing, lowers quality.
- Store at 0° or below.
- Use frozen foods within recommended storage times, to insure maximum quality.

Freezing Particulars

Casseroles: Freeze in foil containers. To heat, uncover and bake. *Or*, line casserole with heavy foil, leaving long ends. Fill. Fold ends of foil together over food to seal. Place container in freezer. Freeze, then remove food from container neatly packaged. (Be sure foil is tightly sealed.) To reheat, place in same casserole.

Meat, poultry, fish: Separate individual portions with 2 sheets of foil or freezer paper so they can be separated while still frozen. Try flattened paper bake cups to separate ground meat patties.

Meat sandwiches: Slice meat loaf or roast beef thin for quick thawing. Lightly butter bread; layer meat generously in each sandwich. To serve, dip frozen sandwiches in egg-and-milk mixture as for French toast; grill about 4 minutes on each side. Serve piping hot.

Gravy: Reheat before freezing; chill. Package and freeze. (Cans are handy.) If gravy (or cream sauce) separates on reheating, beat with fork or spoon.

Spaghetti sauce: Make and freeze sauce. Cook spaghetti at serving time.

Pastry: Stack unbaked pastry rounds flat between waxed paper and freeze.

Marshmallows: Freeze in sealed plastic bag—they won't get brittle. Cut with scissors while freezer-cold—no sticking.

Fruit Freeze: Freeze a can of fruit cocktail. Remove both ends from can; let stand 5 minutes at room temperature. Run spatula around inside of can to loosen, push out. Slice while still icy. Top with whipped cream or mayonnaise.

Cold-plate trick: Chill salad or dessert plates quickly on the freezer shelf.

Top tips: Wrap it right.   Store at 0°.   Use within a few months.

 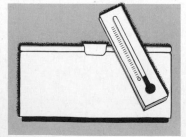 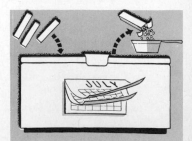

Ready-to-heat meats

Corn-stuffed Pork Chops

4 double-rib pork chops
Salt
½ cup Mexican-style whole kernel corn
½ cup soft bread crumbs
3 tablespoons chopped onions
¼ teaspoon salt
Dash thyme

• • •

¼ teaspoon sage
½ cup hot water

Have meatman cut a pocket in each chop, slitting from fat edge and cutting almost to the bone edge. Salt pocket lightly.

Combine corn, crumbs, onion, salt, and thyme for stuffing; fill pockets in chops. Close openings with toothpicks along fat side. (Insert picks at an angle so they don't keep chops from touching skillet.) Lace with string, if desired.

To freeze: Wrap in moisture-vapor-proof material, separating individual chops with 2 layers of paper; seal tightly. Freeze.

To serve: Unwrap; place in preheated skillet. Sprinkle with sage. Heat slowly till thawed and lightly browned on both sides, about 40 minutes. Add hot water; cover and simmer 40 minutes or till tender. Add more water if necessary. Remove string and picks before serving. Serves 4.

Corned-beef Bunwiches

8 to 10 buns
1 12-ounce can corned beef, shredded
1 cup shredded sharp process American cheese
½ cup chopped stuffed green olives
½ cup catsup
2 tablespoons Worcestershire sauce

Split buns and remove soft centers. Combine remaining ingredients. Fill buns with mixture. Wrap each sandwich separately in foil. Freeze. To serve, heat in moderate oven (375°) 25 minutes or till hot through. Serve with green onions. Serves 8 to 10.

High-hat Meat Loaves

1½ pounds ground beef
1 cup herb-seasoned stuffing mix
1 8-ounce can (1 cup) seasoned tomato sauce
1 slightly beaten egg
1 teaspoon salt
¼ teaspoon pepper

• • •

1 envelope (4 servings) instant mashed or whipped potatoes
Dash paprika
1 medium tomato, cut in 6 wedges
½ cup shredded sharp process cheese

Combine first 6 ingredients. Shape in six 4x2-inch loaves. Place in shallow baking dish (not touching). Cover tightly; freeze.

To serve: Bake covered in moderate oven (350°) 30 minutes. Uncover and continue baking 30 minutes or till done. Remove loaves from oven. Turn oven to 450°. Prepare mashed potatoes according to package directions, but *adding 2 tablespoons additional milk.* Spoon a dollop on each meat loaf. Sprinkle with paprika. Top with tomato wedge; sprinkle with cheese. (See picture on page 52.) Bake 5 to 10 minutes or till potato and tomato are hot. Makes 6 servings.

Jiffy Tuna Skillet

1 medium onion, sliced
1 tablespoon butter or margarine
1 can frozen condensed cream of shrimp soup
½ cup milk
1 cup frozen peas
1 6½-, 7-, or 9¼-ounce can tuna, broken in chunks
Dash pepper

Cook onion in butter till almost tender. Add soup, milk, and peas; cover and heat just to boiling, stirring occasionally. Add tuna and pepper. Heat through. Serve over crisp, oven-warmed chow-mein noodles or hot rice. Makes 4 servings.

Whole meal from freezer

It's company good, too! Team Corn-stuffed Pork Chops with Orange-glazed Yams and tangy Asparagus-Egg Salad. Finale: Walnut Gingerbread with whipped cream.

Fillets Eleganté

Fish never tasted so good! The creamy shrimp sauce adds special flair—you'll think you're eating in a posh restaurant—

> 1 1-pound package frozen
>   fish fillets
>
>   . . .
>
> Fresh-ground pepper
> 2 tablespoons butter or margarine
> 1 can frozen condensed cream
>   of shrimp soup, thawed
> ¼ cup shredded Parmesan cheese
> Paprika

Thaw fish fillets (sole, haddock, halibut, or cod) enough to separate. Arrange in buttered 9-inch pie plate. Dash with pepper and dot with butter or margarine. Spread shrimp soup over fillets and sprinkle with Parmesan cheese and paprika.

Bake at 400° for 25 minutes. Serve with lemon wedges. Makes 4 servings.

Shrimp Curry

> 2 7- or 8-ounce packages frozen
>   shelled shrimp
> 2 tablespoons butter or margarine
> 1½ cups finely chopped pared
>   tart apples
>
>   . . .
>
> 2 tablespoons all-purpose flour
> 2 teaspoons curry powder
> 1 teaspoon salt
> 2 cups milk
> Hot cooked rice

Cook shrimp in boiling water, according to package directions. Drain.

Melt butter; add apples and cook for 5 minutes. Combine the flour, curry powder, and salt; stir into apples. Add milk slowly; cook and stir till sauce is thick. Add shrimp and continue cooking until hot through, stirring occasionally.

Dash curry with paprika; serve with fluffy rice. Makes 5 to 7 servings.

Freezer-easy vegetables

Company Vegetable Bake

2 10-ounce packages frozen peas
 and carrots
1 9-ounce package frozen whole
 green beans
1 5-ounce can water chestnuts,
 drained and sliced
1 3-ounce can (⅔ cup) broiled
 sliced mushrooms, drained

. . .

1 can condensed cream of
 mushroom soup
3 to 4 tablespoons cooking sherry
1 teaspoon Worcestershire sauce
Dash bottled hot pepper sauce
2 cups shredded sharp process
 American cheese
¼ cup rich-round-cracker crumbs

Cook peas and carrots, and beans till just barely tender; drain. Combine with water chestnuts and mushrooms. Combine remaining ingredients, except crumbs, for sauce; toss with vegetables. Turn into a 2-quart casserole.

Bake uncovered at 350° for 40 to 45 minutes, till hot and bubbly. Stir occasionally. Sprinkle with crumbs just before serving. Makes 10 to 12 servings.

Orange-glazed Yams

Open one 14-ounce package frozen candied yams. Leave in carton as directed. Thinly slice ½ orange over yams; drizzle 3 tablespoons orange juice (from ½ orange) over all. Dot with 1 tablespoon butter. Heat yams according to package directions. Makes 3 or 4 servings.

Cheese-topped Potato Patties

Place frozen potato patties from one 12-ounce package on baking sheet. Spread with soft butter. Broil 4 to 5 inches from heat 8 to 10 minutes or till golden brown. Turn; season with salt and pepper.

Sprinkle with ⅓ cup grated sharp process cheese and paprika. Broil 2 to 4 minutes or till cheese melts and browns.

Shrimp Almond Sauce

¼ cup chive cream cheese
¼ cup milk
1 can frozen condensed cream
 of shrimp soup
2 teaspoons lemon juice
2 tablespoons toasted sliced almonds

In saucepan, blend cheese and milk. Add soup. Heat and stir till hot. Add lemon juice; pour over hot cooked broccoli or cauliflower. Sprinkle with almonds. Makes 1½ cups sauce. (See picture, page 4.)

Asparagus-Egg Salad

Cook one 10-ounce package frozen asparagus spears according to package directions; drain. Place in shallow dish.

Combine 2 tablespoons *each* salad oil and vinegar, and 1 teaspoon *each* grated onion and prepared mustard; drizzle over asparagus. Chill well, about 1½ hours.

Slice two hard-cooked eggs; arrange over asparagus (see picture, page 56). Spoon reserved dressing over. Makes 4 servings.

And a bread, too—

Jelly Muffins

1¾ cups sifted all-purpose flour
2 tablespoons sugar
2½ teaspoons baking powder
¾ teaspoon salt
1 well-beaten egg
¾ cup milk
⅓ cup salad oil
Jelly or jam

Sift dry ingredients into bowl; make well in center. Combine egg, milk, and oil. Add all at once to dry ingredients. Stir quickly only till dry ingredients are moistened.

Fill greased muffin pans ⅔ full. Spoon about 1 teaspoon of jelly or jam on top of batter. Wrap and freeze.

To serve, bake (without thawing) at 400° for 25 to 30 minutes or till done.

Dessert at the flip of your freezer door

Hard-to-believe Sherbet

Freeze gelatin and whip. That's all!—

Prepare two 3-ounce packages fruit-flavored gelatin according to package directions. Pour into 1-quart refrigerator tray; freeze firm. Break in small chunks and beat with electric mixer until very smooth. Serve at once. Makes 6 servings.

1-2-3 Strawberry Sherbet

It's super-delicious, full of ripe-berry flavor—

4 cups fresh ripe strawberries
2 cups sugar
2 cups buttermilk

Rinse, drain, and hull strawberries. Add sugar to berries, and mash. Stir in buttermilk. Pour into two 1-quart refrigerator trays; freeze firm.

Break in chunks; beat with electric beater till smooth (or partially freeze and beat smooth with rotary beater). Return to trays; freeze firm. Makes 10 servings.

Lime Ripple Freeze

1 cup packaged corn-flake crumbs or
   4 cups corn flakes, finely crushed
⅓ cup soft butter or margarine
2 tablespoons sugar
1½ pints vanilla ice cream
¼ cup frozen limeade concentrate,
   thawed

Combine crumbs, butter and sugar; mix well. Press over bottom and sides of a 1-quart refrigerator tray; chill.

Stir ice cream to soften. Combine concentrate and few drops green food coloring. Spoon concentrate through ice cream till well marbled; turn into crust. Freeze till firm. Makes 6 to 8 servings.

Raspberry-Lemon Sundaes

1 10-ounce package frozen
   red raspberries
1 pint lemon sherbet

Partially thaw raspberries (they're best to eat while some ice crystals remain). Divide lemon sherbet into 4 sherbet dishes; top with raspberries. Makes 4 servings.

Crunchy Butterscotch Sundaes

1½ cups sugar-coated crisp rice
   or wheat cereal
½ cup flaked coconut
1 quart vanilla ice cream
Butterscotch Sauce

Mix cereal and coconut. Form ice cream in 10 balls; coat with cereal mixture, pressing it on. Place in freezer till serving time. (To keep coating crisp, store only 1 to 4 hours.) Serve with Butterscotch Sauce. Makes 10 servings.

Butterscotch Sauce: Combine 1½ cups brown sugar, ⅔ cup corn syrup, and dash salt. Heat, stirring occasionally, till mixture comes to full boil; cool slightly. Gradually stir in one 6-ounce can evaporated milk. Serve warm or cold.

Cream-cheese Freeze

2 3-ounce packages cream
   cheese, softened
⅔ cup sugar
2½ teaspoons vanilla
2 cups light cream

Cream together the cheese, sugar, and vanilla. Slowly add the cream, mixing thoroughly. Freeze in a 1-quart refrigerator tray till firm. Break in chunks and beat with electric mixer till smooth (or freeze till partially frozen and beat smooth with a rotary beater). Return to tray; freeze firm. Makes 6 servings.

Cream-cheese Freeze— It boasts the "homemade" flavor and creamy smoothness of old-fashioned crank-style ice cream, but it's the simple refrigerator kind! Serve plain or with ripe strawberries.

Pineapple-Coconut Parfaits

It's fluffy frozen pudding ribboned with golden pineapple and coconut—

1 3¼-ounce package coconut-cream pudding
1 cup whipping cream, whipped
1 teaspoon vanilla
2 9-ounce cans (2 cups) crushed pineapple, drained
½ cup flaked coconut
Toasted coconut (optional)

Prepare pudding according to package directions, but using *only 1¾ cups milk;* chill. Beat smooth; then fold in whipped cream and vanilla.

Combine pineapple and coconut. Layer pudding alternately with pineapple mixture in 6 parfait glasses. Sprinkle toasted coconut atop, if desired. Cover tops of glasses with clear plastic wrap or foil; secure "caps" with freezer tape. Freeze.*

Allow parfaits to stand at room temperature about 30 to 40 minutes before serving. Makes 6 servings.

*In a hurry? Omit freezing. Chill, serve.

Tutti-frutti Freeze

Another time, use punch concentrate-pineapple mixture as a sundae sauce—

1 6-ounce can frozen Hawaiian punch concentrate, thawed
1 9-ounce can (1 cup) crushed pineapple, well drained
1 quart vanilla ice cream

Combine punch concentrate and pineapple. Alternate in parfait glasses with ice cream. Freeze. Makes 6 servings. Trim with stems-on maraschino cherries.

Holiday Ice Cream

1 cup prepared mincemeat
1 cup canned jellied cranberry sauce
1 quart vanilla ice cream

Combine mincemeat and cranberry sauce. Stir ice cream just to soften. With spoon, zigzag mincemeat mixture through ice cream to marble. Pile into 1-quart refrigerator tray; freeze firm. Serve in sherbets; stud with toasted almonds. Serves 6 to 8.

Frozen Whipped-cream Toppers

Combine 1 cup whipping cream, ¼ cup confectioners' sugar, and ½ teaspoon vanilla; whip till peaks form. Drop by heaping spoonfuls, several inches apart, onto a chilled baking sheet. Leave tops fluffy or swirl to points with tip of spoon.

Place baking sheet in freezer. When mounds are frozen, use spatula to lift them from cooky sheet. Place in plastic bag; seal tightly and store in freezer till needed. (But use within 3 months.)

Frozen toppers add party touch to desserts. On gingerbread, pie or berries, allow 20 minutes to thaw. For a chilled dessert, thaw the puffs in the refrigerator for 45 minutes to an hour.

Frosty Lemon Fluff

2 egg whites
½ cup sugar
2 egg yolks
½ teaspoon grated lemon peel
¼ cup lemon juice
½ cup whipping cream, whipped
Semisweet-chocolate curls

Beat egg whites till soft peaks form; gradually add sugar, beating to stiff peaks. Beat yolks till thick and lemon colored. Fold yolks, lemon peel, and lemon juice into egg whites. Fold in whipped cream.

Pour into refrigerator tray; freeze firm. Serve in sherbets. Top with shaved chocolate. Makes 6 to 8 servings.

Frozen Rainbow Dessert

1 dozen coconut macaroons
2 cups whipping cream
1 pint *each* lime, raspberry, and
lemon sherbet

Toast macaroons in slow oven (300°) 10 minutes; crush into medium-fine crumbs.

Whip cream just till it *mounds slightly* (not stiff); fold in crumbs. Spread a third of mixture in bottom of 9½x5x3-inch loaf pan. Using *half* of each, quickly spoon sherbets in layers on top. Cover with another third of cream mixture. Repeat layers ending with cream mixture. Freeze firm. Slice. Makes 12 servings.

Lo-cal Lemon Frost

1 egg white
⅓ cup water
⅓ cup nonfat dry milk
1 slightly beaten egg yolk
⅓ cup sugar
¼ teaspoon grated lemon peel
2 to 3 tablespoons lemon juice
Dash salt
3 tablespoons graham-cracker crumbs

Combine egg white, water and dry milk; beat to stiff peaks. Mix next 5 ingredients; gradually beat into egg whites.

Sprinkle *2 tablespoons* of the crumbs into refrigerator tray. Spoon in lemon mixture; dust with crumbs. Freeze. Cut in wedges. Makes 6 servings (80 calories each).

Freezer 3-Fruit Dessert

1 12-ounce package (1½ cups) frozen
   sliced peaches
1 13½-ounce can (1½ cups) frozen
   pineapple chunks
1 tablespoon finely chopped
   candied ginger

    • • •

½ cup fresh blueberries (or use frozen
   blueberries, thawed and drained)

Thaw peaches and pineapple together,
with ginger added. To serve, add blueberries. Spoon into sherbets. Serves 6.

Pink Fruit Freeze: Follow recipe above,
but substitute one 10-ounce package frozen raspberries, thawed, for blueberries.
Omit ginger; dash in aromatic bitters.

Mince Cake Layers

1 sponge-, angel-, or pound-cake
   loaf (about 10x4x2-inches)
1 quart vanilla ice cream
1 cup prepared mincemeat
½ cup slivered blanched
   almonds, toasted
1 teaspoon grated orange peel
1 cup whipping cream, whipped

Rub brown crumbs off cake; cut lengthwise in 3 even layers. Stir ice cream just to
soften. Fold in mincemeat, almonds, and
orange peel; spread between cake layers.
Freeze firm. Before serving, frost top and
sides with whipped cream. Serves 10.

Coconut Praline Cake

⅔ cup brown sugar
⅓ cup butter, melted
¼ cup light cream
1 3½-ounce can flaked coconut
½ teaspoon vanilla

    • • •

Warm 9x9-inch cake

Thoroughly combine first 5 ingredients.
Spread over warm cake. Cool to room temperature. Freeze, then wrap in foil and return to freezer. To serve, remove cake from
freezer; let stand unopened at room temperature about 30 minutes. Remove foil;
broil 5 minutes or till brown and bubbly.

Walnut Gingerbread

⅓ cup shortening
½ cup sugar
1 egg
⅔ cup light molasses
2 cups sifted all-purpose flour
2 teaspoons baking powder
½ teaspoon soda
2 teaspoons ginger
1 teaspoon cinnamon
½ teaspoon salt
¾ cup sour milk
¾ cup chopped walnuts

Stir shortening to soften. Gradually add
sugar; cream well. Add egg and molasses;
beat well. Sift together dry ingredients;
add alternately with sour milk, beating
smooth after each addition. Add nuts. Pour
into well-greased, floured 6½-cup ring.

Bake at 350° 40 to 50 minutes. Cool; remove from mold. Wrap in foil; seal; freeze.
Thaw at room temperature for 1½ hours.

To match picture on page 56; drizzle
with *Orange Icing:* Combine 1 cup sifted
confectioners' sugar with about 4 teaspoons
orange juice. Sprinkle with shredded orange
peel. Place orange-shell flower filled with
whipped cream in center of ring.

Sunday-morning Coffeecake

It's oven-ready, bakes in 25 minutes —

2 tablespoons all-purpose flour
3 tablespoons sugar
½ teaspoon cinnamon
2 tablespoons soft butter
2 tablespoons finely chopped nuts
½ package (1 packet) orange-
   muffin mix
2 tablespoons apricot-pineapple
   preserves (cut up if necessary)

Combine flour, sugar, and cinnamon. Cut
in butter; stir in nuts. Prepare muffin mix
according to package directions.

Spoon batter into greased 8-inch round
cake pan (or use foil pan). Sprinkle crumb
topping over; dot with preserves. Cover
tightly with foil; freeze.*

To serve, bake *frozen* cake at 400° for 25
minutes. Cut in wedges; serve warm.

*Or, bake immediately at 400° for 18 to
20 minutes; cool. Then, wrap; freeze. To
serve, heat *frozen* cake in hot oven (400°)
15 minutes or till warm through.

Index